CHILDREN ACT
and
SCHOOLS

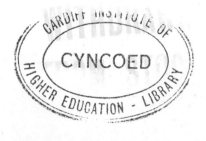

Kogan Page Books for Teachers series
Series Editor: Tom Marjoram

The
CHILDREN ACT
and
SCHOOLS

A Guide to Good Practice

BEN WHITNEY

KOGAN PAGE

London • Philadelphia

For Jo and David –
Who are thoroughly sick of The Children Act!

First published in 1993
Reprinted 1994

Kogan Page Limited
120 Pentonville Road
London N1 9JN

© Ben Whitney, 1993

British Library Cataloguing in Publication Data

A CIP record for this book is available from the British Library

ISBN 0 7494 1115 5

Typeset by DP Photosetting, Aylesbury, Bucks
Printed and bound in Great Britain by
Biddles Ltd, Guildford and King's Lynn

Contents

The Children Act and Schools

Acknowledgements

My thanks are due to colleagues in numerous schools and in Staffordshire Education Welfare Service, in particular Francis Luckcock and Andrew Pointon, Principal Education Welfare Officer, who have been a constant source of encouragement. The opinions expressed, however, are my own and do not necessarily reflect the policy of the service or the education authority.

Ben Whitney
Summer 1993

Introduction

THE CHILDREN ACT AND EDUCATION REFORM

'Not another law telling teachers what to do! Surely we've got far too much to handle already?' I can hear the protests from my own teacher friends and colleagues ringing in my ears even as I start! I have every sympathy with them, but I hope I can convince you that this law is different.

The Children Act 1989 is not an Act about education. There have been quite enough of those in recent years, including the longest one ever in 1993. These have gradually brought about the implementation of the proposals outlined in the 'Parent's Charter' and, even allowing for disputes along the way and possible changes of government in the future, such reforms can rightly be seen as laying the foundations for educational provision for the next generation.

The Children Act is doing the same for the welfare of children in England and Wales. It has made fundamental changes to the way in which our society will go about addressing their needs for the foreseeable future. That, at least, was the Government's stated intention when the Act became law in October 1991.

There are those who argue that many of its aims will never become reality and there is some justification for this scepticism. Some of the Act's expectations are already proving unrealistic or too radical to escape dilution as more punitive ideas begin to take hold again. But the vast majority of its provisions are surely here to stay and, for countless children – far more than those who will need their problems addressing through much-publicized changes to the juvenile justice system – the Children Act provides the context for ensuring that they are properly cared for within their families and communities.

It is not always easy to reconcile the expectations of the Act against those arising from recent educational changes. Its commitment to promoting the welfare of *all* children may not sit too easily with a market economy within schools where the emphasis is on competition, performance and success. Under this philosophy, some children become a liability. The Government has already had to act to ensure that our city centres are not filled with young people who, far from 'truanting', are actually permanently excluded from the mainstream educational process as unwanted and unmanageable. It is hard to see that education reform will lead to a better deal for children like these.

Schools tend to be hierarchical and highly managed institutions in which the principles of listening to the views of children and taking their wishes and feelings into account are rarely formalized in procedures and practice. Of course all schools seek to be caring, pastoral communities, but the 'welfare' approach is sometimes seen as too 'soft' in contrast to the expectations of self-discipline and conformity which are inevitably at the heart of most schools. There is often very little apparent incentive for staff to take the extra time and trouble such an alternative approach requires, especially when under so much pressure from other demands and expectations.

So why is it important that teachers and their managers should be familiar with the provisions of the Children Act? Wouldn't it be better to keep a clear distinction between the Department of Health and the Department for Education and recognize that these legislative priorities are simply irreconcilable? There are several reasons why those concerned for the proper education of children cannot choose that easy option.

Schools are for children

It is fashionable these days to talk of parents as the consumers of education. They do make important choices and are those to whom schools have a duty to be accountable. But that makes children the 'product', when in reality it is the *children* who are the customers and education itself which is the product. We need a reminder of this; that the needs of children must be at the heart of what we do and why we do it. Governors have sometimes said to me, in response to a training presentation on the Act, that it's nice to talk about the pupils for a change rather than just approaching the school as if it were a small business. Teachers with whom I have worked have welcomed the opportunity afforded by the Act to promote a more holistic view of children and their needs within the educational process. The

Children Act provides an excellent way of focusing our priorities and enabling children to take centre stage in our thinking as they surely should.

Parents are our partners

Yet, of course, it is impossible to move in education without reference to parents. They have a wide range of rights and responsibilities. They may participate in the management of their children's school to the point of sharing in making the appointment of the headteacher, voting for representatives on the governing body or deciding whether the school will continue to be maintained by the LEA. Consultation evenings, written reports and assessments, brochures and league tables, all these are proliferating at a frantic rate as governors and teachers fulfil their legal duties to treat parents with ever greater care. But how do schools know who their parents are?

The significance of the Children Act is that it has effectively redefined what is meant by the term 'parent', including a specific amendment to the 1944 Education Act and all subsequent legislation arising from it. In particular, it has radically changed the position of divorced and separated parents who do not live with their child. Policy makers and practitioners in schools cannot possibly be confident that they have fulfilled their legal obligations towards parents unless they have recognized the significance of these changes. Parents are entitled to have a clear grasp of their rights and responsibilities under the Children Act in order to be sure that they are receiving proper attention from their children's school. They have a right to information about how to secure their legal status where this is an issue. These questions could affect up to half of the children in some schools and cannot be ignored by those responsible for home–school liaison if our practice is to reflect the reality of children's family life.

Agencies must work together

Schools form the largest agency that works with children; they are a vital link in procedures for child protection. Education is given a key place in the Children Act as a highly significant part of a child's life which must be taken into account when a decision is being made about his welfare. Dealing with absence from school is given a new impetus by provision within the Act which requires inter-agency consultation first. It also lays a duty upon local authority departments – Education, Social Services, Health and Housing – to co-operate in ensuring that services are made available to parents and their children in ways which support and encourage family life. Although it is LEAs rather than schools which are explicitly given this responsibility, in the current climate of local financial management and the growth of the grant maintained sector, this duty must inevitably devolve to school staff as well as to education welfare officers/education social workers.

THE AIMS OF THIS BOOK

In theory and in practice, it is impossible for schools to separate themselves from the general movement in society to address the welfare needs of children. Teachers cannot operate in a vacuum, pursuing their own objectives with the same children who, elsewhere in their lives, are subject to, and empowered by, the most wide-ranging reform of the law about children this century. If education is to take its proper place as central to the process of enabling children to develop into mature citizens, schools need to take account of the whole range of their needs and gifts. The Children Act has made it clear that there is no 'educational' part which can be addressed independently of everything else, just for the time that children are at school. This book details how the Act has done this and what difference it makes.

The guidance given here arises out of numerous training presentations for schools during 1991–93 and is based on extensive practical experience of dealing with enquiries direct from staff and parents. It is intended to help teachers, governors, education welfare officers, social workers, parents and children themselves to respond to the issues which the Children Act raises for schools. It touches on a wide range of everyday situations within school life from the involvement of parents to dealing with absences, all of which are radically affected by the Act. Pastoral staff in particular need to be familiar with these changes but anyone with tutorial or managerial responsibilities will need to re-examine their practice and policy.

Much of the Act can be put on one side as not directly relevant. But some parts are absolutely essential – without them headteachers, governors and staff risk not only poor practice but ill-informed decisions which could have considerable legal repercussions. The primary aim of this book is to select those parts which are of special relevance within schools and steer a path through the minefield for the mutual benefit of everyone involved.

Please note that the use of the male gender throughout when talking about children is intended to include both boys and girls.

Legislation still uses 'he' and for me to do otherwise would only cause confusion. The word 'child' is normally used to cover all under-18s, as the Act, unlike previous provision, does not use the term 'young person' for older children.

1

The Children Act 1989

WHY CHILDREN NEEDED A NEW LAW

Public and private law

When the Children Act was passing through Parliament in 1989 it received all-party support and was widely recognized as a major step forward in ensuring the welfare and safety of children in our society. Despite a general lack of publicity at the time, probably because it was not a party-political issue, specialist commentators and legislators described the Act as a substantial reform which would have wide-ranging implications. It fully repeals or partially replaces a considerable amount of previous legislation and changes some well-entrenched practices and ideas. Why was it necessary to have such an overhaul of the law? What was going wrong?

For some years there had been increasing concern about the welfare of children on two fronts, usually described under the headings of 'public' and 'private' law. While these terms have no official validity, they do provide a useful way of distinguishing between a range of legal provisions which may be of significance in a child's life. What is unique about the Act is that it undertook a harmonization of the law across this wide spectrum so that now, whether it is private or public law which is being used, it is the Children Act which is the framework for determining what will happen.

Public law relates to all those areas where society has a need to intervene in the life of a child or family through the courts or the local authority. Care proceedings; child protection; children who need to live away from home; children who are having difficulty attending school – prior to the Children Act a range of laws and statutes might be used in all these areas, some dating back almost half a century. Action would take place in the juvenile court, alongside children in trouble for committing offences.

Private law relates to areas of dispute about children within the family, especially in the context of their parents' separation or divorce. Here too care and supervision orders might have been made, but under entirely different legislation from that which operated under public law. These and other orders would be made in domestic proceedings in a county divorce court, often involving the same children who might be the subject of other proceedings in other courts.

Throughout the 1980s a number of reports and reviews, in both the public and the private law sectors, and from both Parliament and the Law Commission, led to an acceptance of the need for a more coherent body of law which would apply to all children in whatever context a decision was needed about their welfare. This long process culminated in a draft of a Children Bill, covering a reform of the private law to which additional clauses were then added covering public law issues (see figure 1.1).

It is essential to recognize that the first 16 sections of the Act, which are virtually the same as the draft Bill, set the tone for the whole of the rest. These deal with a new way of settling issues within the family and are the basic building blocks on which the Act is constructed. In that sense it is best to see the private law aspects as fundamental, not only in terms of the numbers of children likely to be affected, but also in terms of principle. The Act is essentially about the family; about *all* children and their parents. Public provision for children in difficulty is then set against this basic context. Not all professionals in social work and elsewhere seem to have understood the significance of this.

In many ways the legislation was overtaken by events and the public law aspects became highlighted in an unexpected way. By the time the Act passed through Parliament, and certainly by the time it was implemented in October 1991, public concern had become focused much more on the public law than had been the case originally. The events in Cleveland, where large numbers of children were removed from their parents on suspicion of sexual abuse, and the subsequent Butler-Sloss report, had led to widespread anxiety about social workers overstepping their responsibilities and intervening too readily into the privacy of family life. This tied in with the generally less interventionist tone of the original Bill, and subsequent events such as the 'pindown' inquiry and further examples of excessive intervention in Rochdale and elsewhere, only served to reinforce this opinion that new procedures were needed.

The Children Act 1989

PUBLIC LAW

83 Social Services
    Committee Report
    "Children in Care"
    |
84 Review of Child
    Care Law
    |
87 White Paper:
    "Child Care and
    Family Services"

PRIVATE LAW

Law Commission Reports:
85 Guardianship
85 Custody
87 Orders in Custody
    Proceedings
    |
88 Report on Guardianship
    and Custody
    (incl. draft of
    Children Bill)

(88 Cleveland
Report)

Children Act 1989
(October 14th 1991)

fully repeals: Custody of Children Act 1891
    Nurseries and Child Minders
    Regulations Act 1948
    Guardianship of Minors Act 1971
    Children Act 1975
    Child Care Act 1980
    Foster Children Act 1980
    Children's Homes Act 1982

plus large
parts of: C and YP Act 1963
    C and YP Act 1969
    Adoption Act 1976
    plus others

Figure 1.1 *Children Act – origins*

An Act for all agencies

This emphasis on the public law prompted initial thoughts that the Act was really only of any significance for Social Services Departments and that other agencies which work with children, especially schools, need not give it much attention. Councils gave SSDs significant extra resources to enable them to meet the requirements of the Act – and rightly so. The Act places a wide range of new powers and duties on them, especially in connection with day care for children under eight and the monitoring of children's welfare in residential settings, as well as reinforcing responsibilities for child protection, children who need looking after and children 'in need'. Of course SSDs are the lead agency in implementing its provisions. But there has been rather less awareness of the private law implications, especially the effects of the new concept of 'parental responsibility' and how other agencies might also need to adapt their practice in response to the Act.

I can still recall a social worker colleague telling me that there was only one section of the Act which need concern education welfare and little preparation was offered either to schools or to educational professionals in the early days. The Open University training material on the Act, which was used extensively in local authorities and by magistrates before October 1991, scarcely mentions the fact that children go to school! It seriously under-represents the role of education services in promoting the welfare of children. No doubt this was because it was the DoH which was making the running (and, presumably, providing the funding).

The OU/DfE subsequently had to produce material dealing with the Act's educational implications in isolation which, while welcome, was very much a second-best procedure and hardly in keeping with the inter-agency approach laid down by the Act itself. This has been a continuing problem in recent years. Most reviews of the Act in operation have focused only on how Social Services practice has changed and many books and commentaries have seen education as affected only by education supervision orders.

But the roots of the Act betray this overemphasis on the public law and there are *two* distinct reasons why it was felt that children needed a new law: the abuse of power and family breakdown.

Responding to the abuse of power

Non-intervention

It is right to see the Children Act as a significant reduction in the power of agencies and this has had a major impact, not only in SSDs, but also in the ways of working now adopted by education welfare/ education social work services (see figure 1.2). Although I have sometimes found that headteachers and others find this point uncomfortable, the Act does not give a fresh range of powers to local authorities and LEAs with which they can tackle children's problems through the courts. There *are* new provisions, but most of them are less interventionist than before and require a clear threshold to be reached before they can be justified. In general the Act has empowered parents, the courts and, to some extent, children

Why children needed a new law

Responding to the abuse of power

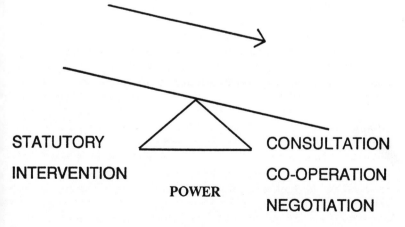

AGENCIES

PROFESSIONALS

INSTITUTIONS

PARENTS

COURTS

CHILDREN

STATUTORY

INTERVENTION

POWER

CONSULTATION

CO-OPERATION

NEGOTIATION

Figure 1.2 *Why children needed a new law (1)*

themselves, and disempowered professionals, agencies and institutions.

This fits within the Government's general philosophy, seen more clearly in education than perhaps anywhere else, of giving parents more say with respect to their children's lives. 'Parents know best' as regards the welfare of their own children. Courts, rather than agencies, are given the role of guarding the welfare of children *in extremis* and acting as the arbiters in disputes, either between parents, or between parents and professionals. It is much more of an open question than it used to be whether courts will back what an agency wants to do. Only a court can now decide that parents have sufficiently failed to secure the welfare of their child, or that they pose them sufficient threat, to justify intervention on a statutory basis. It *was* too easy to obtain the necessary authority in the past. It was then too difficult for parents to challenge those decisions and it took too long before new decisions could be made giving parents control again. All that has changed dramatically.

To give an example most relevant to education, a child can no longer be made the subject of a care order because he is not going to school. Children cannot be 'removed' from their parents on grounds of truancy or 'sent away' as a punishment. Not going to school might still be part of the concern being expressed about a child, and part of the basis for action by the SSD where a child is suffering, or at risk of, 'significant harm', but the LEA's powers under the Children Act are now more limited than before (see Chapter 4).

The rights of the child

The empowerment of children has been more controversial, though it has not yet had much impact outside the sphere of residential care and private law issues. Neither is it quite as extensive as is sometimes claimed. There was much media attention in the early days about children having the right to 'divorce' their parents or being allowed to run riot in children's homes without anyone having the right to restrain them. The latter issue has now been addressed by new guidance from the DoH, but the first was largely an exaggerated media-generated misunderstanding, fuelled by examples from the USA of something quite different.

The Children Act does not give children the right to 'divorce' their parents, nor even to be heard directly if their parents are divorcing each other. It does give them the right (some would say too restricted a right), if they can convince a court that they understand what they are doing, to make applications for the resolution of disputes about, for example, where they should live. It does not mean they will always get what they want; but the Act does give children a right to be consulted and listened to when certain decisions about their lives are being made, and, with increasing maturity, there are increasing opportunities for children to take up a point of view different from that of their parents, social worker or teacher. It should come as no surprise that they sometimes do so.

Working by agreement
All this has led to a major shift in the way in which agencies now seek to work with children and their parents. The key word is 'partnership'. Social work involvement is only rarely based on a duty to enforce statutory orders. Such a duty would, if required, represent the end of a very long road in which all possible attempts must first be made to resolve problems by consultation, negotiation and agreement. Even where there is concern about a child protection issue, parents and, where appropriate, children, must be fully involved in determining what is going to happen. All possible ways will be explored of resolving the problems by voluntary means, which, in the vast majority of cases, will be all that is needed. Orders will only be sought if they would be of positive benefit to the child and no other resolution is possible.

This 'no order' principle, which applies equally in public and private law proceedings, has meant that far less use has been made of courts and far more effort made to find innovative ways of enabling parents, children and professionals to work together. The number of care orders made, for example, has fallen dramatically, as has the number of times orders have been used for child protection. There is, as yet, no evidence that this has led to an unacceptable risk to children, though society may have to accept that there is some price to be paid for an approach which allows a greater element of privacy in family life and keeps professionals at arm's length.

So, again in an educational context, education welfare officers/education social workers should seek to do everything they can to resolve, for example, a child's non-attendance at school, without resorting to the courts. Written agreements, consultation meetings with parents and children present, voluntary packages of action involving give and take on all sides, are all becoming more common and will continue to do so. There is, in reality, no 'big stick' which can be brought out to frighten children into doing as they are told. Even court action under the Children Act is not to be seen as punishment and proceedings in a magistrates' court against parents for failing to ensure that their children are properly educated do not involve the child at all.

Even if such action is taken, parents and children will still be encouraged to participate in the decision-making wherever possible and every opportunity taken to avoid the use of courts. This does not always sit too comfortably with the DfE's expectations of early prosecution, or with an overemphasis on professional expertise and authority, but the Children Act must set the boundaries where the welfare of children is concerned. This may, however, lead to some of them, especially older children, apparently falling through the net where little progress is being made voluntarily but the use of statutory powers is still not possible or appropriate.

This is inevitable. Keeping the power with the parents and recognizing that young people have rights to have some say over what happens in their own lives means that no one may have the authority to enforce changes unless they are absolutely necessary. Some children will 'get away' with school refusal because persuasion cannot win them over and no statutory alternatives are available. Society has not given its agencies the powers to resolve *all* problems. The state is not all- powerful, and few would wish it to be so.

Responding to family breakdown

The reality of family life
The second context out of which change has come is the dramatically changed state of the family in British society (see figure 1.3). School governors have a duty under the Pupils' Registration (Amendment) Regulations 1988 to draw up a register of 'every person known to the proprietor of the school to be a parent of each child registered at the school' in order to identify to whom the rights and responsibilities detailed in the 'Parent's Charter' should be offered. (With the 1993 Education Act these become 'registered parents' for grant-maintained ballot purposes.) But it is simply no longer possible to assume, as some schools may have done in the past, that 'parents' automatically means the two people living at home with the child and that all children live in conventional nuclear families.

The statistics speak for themselves in terms of the numbers of children likely to be caught up in the consequences of the breakdown of their parents' relationship. Many children live with only one parent with the other absent or live as part of two families with a range of parental figures in each. Many live with people other than their actual parents who may themselves be living in a variety of relationships which are frequently changing. This is the reality of

Why children needed a new law

Responding to family breakdown

180,000 divorces a year

1.3 million one-parent families

700,000 children losing touch with a parent

'absent' parents not accepting
responsibility (Child Support Agency 1993)

BUT RECOGNISING THAT SOCIETY IS CHANGING
A new concept of the 'family'

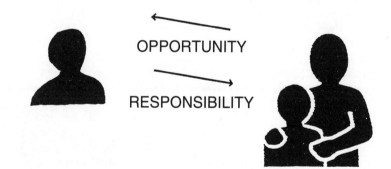

Figure 1.3 *Why children needed a new law (2)*

family life for countless children and, although reform of the divorce law may mean some changes, this is an irreversible trend for the foreseeable future with which schools in particular have to come to terms.

The Children Act recognizes this reality without condemnation, but it recognizes too that much of the response to this situation in the past tended to make things worse for the children. In the context of growing concern about juvenile crime in 1993 there was much talk of the need for some kind of inquiry or even a Royal Commission into the state of the family. But we have already had it and the Children Act is the result. Although not generally appreciated, the Act is seeking to establish, in the words of one of the information booklets published by the DoH, nothing less than 'a new code of law about the upbringing of children to ensure that we achieve the very best for this and for future generations'. (*The Children Act and the Courts – a Guide for Parents*, DoH, 1991. See Appendix 2.) It was needed because there was widespread feeling that the law was failing to provide children with proper support in facing the consequences of change in their families.

'Absent' parents

One problem in particular was often the focus of concern: that far too many children were losing touch with one or other of their parents, either as a result of public law proceedings, such as the making of a care order, or, far more frequently, following divorce proceedings in which one parent was awarded 'custody, care and control' and the other 'access'. This tended to foster both the abdication of responsibility by the non-custodial parent and the loss of that relationship for the child. The whole philosophy encouraged an adversarial contest in which the winner took all and the loser dropped out.

Despite research which indicated that children do best when a relationship with *each* parent is sustained after a separation, the organization 'Families Need Fathers' estimated in 1992 that there were upwards of 700,000 children who had entirely lost touch with one or other of their parents. Children in care ended up dependent on the local authority which had 'won' control of them and taken their parents' rights away. Inevitably they tended then to remain in care for a long time and have no family to return to afterwards. 'Absent' parents tended to see little obligation to support their children financially once the system had said to them that they were no longer required as a significant parental figure in their children's lives. The Children Act is, in a sense, the other side of the Child

Support Act – more pay should mean more say; with responsibility should come opportunity.

This problem was nowhere more evident than in schools where parents who did not live with their children would frequently be excluded from decision-making about their lives or receive little information about their progress. The DfE's guidance on parental involvement suggested that non-custodial parents could effectively be by-passed after the minimum of effort on the school's part (advice which, incidentally, was still circulating long after the Children Act had become law).

Schools would rarely ask for details of a child's family history; they would accept whatever they were told by the person admitting the child and so would often collude, albeit inadvertently, in ensuring that one parent was effectively kept in the dark. Reports would normally be sent home with the children but nowhere else; invitations to meetings and consultation evenings would reach only those who had day-to-day care of the child, even in situations where the child still had an active relationship with the other parent, though often, of course, outside the Monday to Friday school timetable. All this tended to encourage the very thing which society believed to be a problem – the abdication of parental responsibility and a massive growth in the problems arising from children growing up with insecure parental relationships.

Responsible parenthood
What is offered in the Children Act is a new understanding of the family, not only in terms of the complexity of many children's lives but also recognizing that people do not necessarily have to live together in order to form a network of significant relationships. The Act asks whether the ending of the parents' relationship with each other must necessarily mean the ending of responsible parenthood. Surely it is realistic to ask parents to arrange things so that, wherever reasonably possible and preferably by agreement and negotiation rather than orders, *both* of them will sustain involvement with their children, even if they no longer wish to be a couple? Their own relationship is an entirely different issue from their continuing joint responsibility towards their children. 'One-parent family' is a misleading phrase if what has actually happened is that the two parents have simply chosen to live apart. No one has ceased to be a parent by such a decision.

The Act seeks to encourage a longer-term view; to recognize that arrangements which are made now, for example about where a child will live or whether he needs to be in care, might not necessarily be in his best interests at some point in the future. It is important to keep all options open, to sustain all the possibilities so that later, perhaps in response to the growing child's own wishes, changes could be made. People who have been left on one side 10 years earlier are no longer there when the teenager needs them and society is constantly having to face the consequences of such lost contacts. Crucially, the Act asks for honesty, which appears not to be a regular feature of the way in which many families handle broken relationships. Everyone, including the child, should be clear about who is responsible for him so that he can grow up fully aware of his past history, with no sudden surprises which betray his trust or which leave him confused and angry.

Because of their commitment to children's wellbeing, school staff are uniquely placed to be at the forefront of ensuring that these more open possibilities become reality. If 'absent' parents are not accepted as active partners in their children's education, it is not likely that they will feel valued and accepted at all and children will continue to lose touch with them. What happens in schools will be one of the key tests of whether the Children Act is working, not just for those few children who are subject to public law proceedings, but for the vast numbers of children who have experienced breakdown and loss within their family. This is a crucial challenge for schools; there is still a long way to go to meet it.

THE ACT IN SUMMARY

The Children Act 1989 is a substantial piece of legislation with 108 sections, 15 accompanying Schedules and 9 volumes of detailed guidance. By normal standards it is remarkably clearly written and easy to use, even though it was allegedly drafted by a middle-aged bachelor! This summary is not an exhaustive guide but it seeks to highlight those aspects of the Act which are of particular significance for school-aged children, and therefore, for schools (see figure 1.4).

Part 1 Introduction

s1   The welfare of the child
The welfare of the child is 'paramount' when a court determines any question with respect to the upbringing of a child or the administration of his property. Delay is to be avoided and courts will only make an order on the basis that it is better for the child than making no order. Section 1 (3) contains the 'welfare checklist', a list of criteria

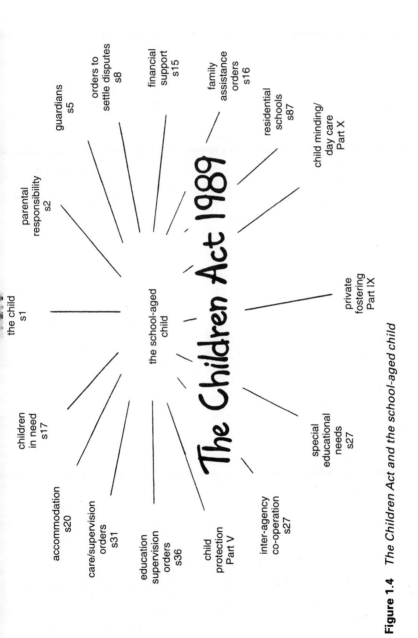

Figure 1.4 *The Children Act and the school-aged child*

which a court must apply in most decisions under the Act (though not all), including most public law applications and private law disputes:

(a) 'the ascertainable wishes and feelings of the child concerned (considered in the light of his age and understanding);

(b) his physical, emotional and educational needs;

(c) the likely effect on him of any changes in his circumstances;

(d) his age, sex, background and any characteristics of his which the court considers relevant;

(e) any harm he has suffered or is at risk of suffering;

(f) how capable each of his parents, and any other person in relation to whom the court considers the question to be relevant, is of meeting his needs;

(g) the range of powers available to the court under this Act in the proceedings in question.'

s2   Parental responsibility for children

Parental responsibility is held by both parents if married at the time the child is born; if they are unmarried it is held only by the mother unless the father acquires it. People do not lose parental responsibility because someone else acquires it and each person may act alone and without the other in meeting it, provided this is not incompatible with an existing order. People with parental responsibility may not surrender or transfer it, though they can arrange for others to carry it out on their behalf, without affecting their liability. This does not, however, actually give that other person parental responsibility in their own right. (Parental responsibility continues until a child is 18 and can *only* be lost by adoption once held as of right.)

s3   Meaning of parental responsibility

'All the rights, duties, powers, responsibilities and authority which by law a parent has in relation to the child and his property.' Whether or not someone has parental responsibility does not affect any other obligations which they may have towards the child (eg, to ensure that they are properly educated or to maintain them financially). People who do not have parental responsibility, but do have care of the child, may, subject to the provisions of the Act, do what is reasonable to safeguard and promote their welfare.

s4   Acquisition of parental responsibility by father

An unmarried father can obtain parental responsibility by application for an order, or, provided it is on the prescribed form, by making an agreement with the mother if she is willing. Orders and agreements can only be ended by the court. (An unmarried father who subsequently marries the mother obtains parental responsibility *de facto*.)

ss5–6 *Guardians*
Guardians only take effect where there is no one with parental responsibility left alive, or where the parent who has died has a sole residence order (see s8 below). Guardians acquire parental responsibility on taking up the guardianship. It can be ended by a court. Guardians must be appointed, in writing, in advance, but the appointment only takes effect on the parents' death.

s7 *Welfare reports*
Courts may call for reports from probation officers and local authorities to help them determine a question with respect to a child. They may ask others to assist them.

Part II Orders with respect to children in family proceedings

ss8–11 *Residence, contact and other orders*
These orders replace custody and access orders. They may be made in existing disputes, by application by certain categories of person, and in both public and private law proceedings. Section 8 orders normally end when the child is 16 unless the circumstances are exceptional.

Residence Order: an order settling the arrangements to be made as to the person with whom the child is to live;

Contact Order: an order requiring the person with whom a child lives to allow them to visit, stay with, or otherwise have contact with, the person named in the order;

Prohibited Steps Order: an order that no step which may be taken by a parent in meeting their parental responsibility and which is specified in the order, may be taken by any person without the consent of the court;

Specific Issue Order: an order giving directions for the purpose of determining a specific question which has arisen in connection with any aspect of parental responsibility for a child.

s12 *Residence orders and parental responsibility*
Where the court makes a residence order in favour of any person,

that person acquires parental responsibility for the child while the order remains in force, if they do not have it already. (Unlike adoption, this does not remove parental responsibility from anyone else who has it.)

s13   Change of child's name/removal from jurisdiction
Where a residence order is in force, a child may not be known by a new surname or removed from the United Kingdom (except for up to one month by the person(s) named on the order), without the written consent of *all* those with parental responsibility or leave of the court.

s14   Enforcement of residence orders

s15   Orders for financial relief

s16   Family assistance orders
New orders (replacing matrimonial supervision orders) which allow a court to direct that parents and children co-operate with a probation officer or other officers of the local authority for up to six months in order to resolve a dispute about the child's welfare.

Part III Local authority support for children and families

s17   Provision of services for children in need
Local authorities have a duty 'to promote and safeguard the welfare of children in need in their area and, so far as is consistent with that duty, to promote the upbringing of such children by their families'. This should be by the provision of a range of services as set out in Schedule 2. They must also facilitate the provision of such services by others, including in particular, voluntary organizations. Assistance may be in kind and, in exceptional circumstances, in cash. 'Children in need' includes those 'unlikely to achieve or maintain a reasonable standard of health and development; children whose health and development (including intellectual, physical, emotional, social or behavioural development) is, or is likely to be, significantly impaired, and children who are disabled'.

ss18–19   Day care for pre-school and other children
Focused especially on children in need and covering a duty to provide supervised activities for children outside school hours and in school holidays. To be reviewed on an inter-agency basis every three years.

ss20–21   Provision of accommodation for children
The replacement for 'voluntary care'. One of a range of services to help parents of children in need.

ss22–24   General duties with respect to 'looked after' children
Children are looked after if they are accommodated by any local authority, health authority, LEA etc or if they are 'in care' (see s31 below). These sections set out the detailed arrangements including duties on the various agencies to liaise with each other and the duty on the local authority to offer all such children assistance when they are no longer looked after but under 21.

s25   Use of accommodation for restricting liberty
Regulations covering the circumstances under which children may be placed in secure accommodation by order from the court.

s26   Power to review children being looked after

s27   Co-operation between authorities
Local authorities (including education, health, housing etc) have a *duty* to co-operate with each other in providing services to children in need. Local authorities must assist the LEA with the provision of services to children with special educational needs, eg joint assessments. (s27(4) and Schedule 2.3, now replaced by s166 Education Act 1993 and includes District Health Authorities.)

ss28–30   Consultation procedures/miscellaneous provisions

Part IV Care and supervision

ss31–32   Care and supervision orders
Can be made only on the application of the local authority (SSD) or the NSPCC to the court. Based on the child suffering, or being likely to suffer, 'significant harm' and that the care being given to him is not reasonable or he is beyond parental control. These are the *only* grounds for care proceedings (ie, non-attendance at school, or 'moral danger' no longer exist as grounds). Only children on a care order are 'in care'.

ss33–35   Effects of care and supervision orders
The local authority acquires parental responsibility on the making of a care order (in addition to anyone who already has it). Contact with parents may be restricted.

s36   Education supervision orders
A new power for the LEA to apply to have a child placed under its supervision for up to one year where he is 'not being properly educated' and is of compulsory school age. (Detailed provision in Schedule 3.)

ss37–40   Powers of the court; interim orders etc

ss41–42   Guardians ad litem
An independent person may be appointed to represent the child's interests in court proceedings. They have right of access to local authority records about the child.

Part V Child protection

s43   Child assessment orders
Short-term orders (seven days) which require a person who is in a position to produce the child to make him available for an assessment to determine whether he is suffering, or likely to suffer, significant harm. There is no change in parental responsibility and the child may only be kept away from home as specified in the order.

ss44–45   Emergency protection orders
Orders for crisis situations only, where the child needs immediate protection (replacing the place of safety order). The applicant (can be anyone but will be the SSD or NSPCC in practice) acquires parental responsibility for the duration of the order. Lasts for eight days (may be extended up to 15 maximum). Keeping a child away from home longer would require an application for an interim care order.

s46   Removal and accommodation of children by the Police
Short-term orders (72 hours) SSD must be informed.

s47   Local authority duty to investigate
Duty to make enquiries when there is reasonable cause to suspect that a child is suffering, or is likely to suffer, significant harm. Duty to consult with the LEA where applicable and duty on LEA to assist.

ss48–52   Various powers/recovery of abducted children etc

Part VI Community homes

ss53–58   Regulations concerning local authority homes

Part VII Voluntary homes/voluntary organizations

ss59–62   Regulation/registration of voluntary homes etc

Part VIII Registered children's homes

ss63–65   Regulations to promote the welfare of children in homes

Part IX Private fostering

ss66–70   Regulations/offences etc

Part X Child minding/day care for young children

ss71–79   Regulations concerning children under eight
Often interpreted to include children under 10. Young children who are cared for in a school's summer holiday scheme may come within the scope of these regulations. SSDs are responsible for registration and inspection. Schools as such are exempt.

Part XI Powers of the Secretary of State

ss80–84   Department of Health responsibilities
Includes power to inspect accommodation in residential schools, hold enquiries, etc.

Part XII Miscellaneous and general

ss85–108   Various provisions
Includes regulations concerning the welfare of children looked after by LEAs and in independent boarding schools and various provisions concerning court hearings etc. 'Family proceedings' are now separate from criminal proceedings and can be heard at and transferred between any level of court (magistrates', county, high). The proceedings are confidential and no information may be published which might identify a child, including, for example, the school they attend.

Sch12.4   Abolition of imprisonment for parental failure to ensure that children are properly educated.

Sch13   Detailed provision concerning the prosecution of parents under the 1944 Education Act (now the 1993 Act). The amendment of the definition of 'parent' to include both someone who is not a

parent of a child but has parental responsibility for him and someone who has care of him.

Sch14.6   Specifies that where parents were married when the child'
was born and there are existing orders with respect to the child (eg,
'custody, care and control' to one parent), *each* parent now has
parental responsibility for him.

2

Working Together for the Welfare of Children

CHILD PROTECTION

A new approach

Promoting the welfare of children within schools is about much more than child protection, but this is a good place to start as it is an important statutory responsibility on staff and governors which has been sharpened by the Children Act. It is best not to think of this issue in terms of 'child abuse' but to take the more positive view indicated by 'child protection'. School staff are essential partners in ensuring both that children are properly protected from potential abuse and, when problems have arisen, that clear inter-agency plans are carried through to offer the child continued protection. The Children Act has changed the range of orders available to the SSD or the NSPCC (see Part V of the summary of the Act). In general, orders are more difficult to obtain and last for a much shorter period of time. This, however, is not the most important information for schools as very few children require the making of orders. It is the changes in philosophy which have most impact and they may be summarized as follows:

(a) The emphasis is more clearly on the welfare of the child rather than necessarily assuming that removing the child from their family unit is the almost inevitable consequence of the investigation and response. That may do the child more harm than good. It should be just as likely, for example, that the alleged abuser will leave the family home, thereby ensuring that the child is protected but with the minimum of disruption to his normal life, especially his education. The Act allows local authorities to pay for adults

35

to be accommodated away from home in such circumstances, though some court rulings have still tended to assume children's removal into care. Such decisions are, however, hotly contested by the SSDs involved as being against both the letter and the spirit of the Act.

(b)   There should be far less pressure to use statutory powers and to seek court orders unless the needs of the child require it. In line with the general principle of working co-operatively wherever possible, professionals will normally seek ways of responding to the alleged abuse which protect the child by negotiation and agreement. There is no need for the stigmatizing and intrusive process of orders unless there is no alternative. (It is important to be clear that not all proven incidents of abuse will necessarily end up as criminal matters, even if proceedings are required under the Children Act. Different thresholds may apply in terms of the necessary levels of evidence required.)

(c)   Children's own views and wishes should be taken into account more carefully. This is reflected of course in the importance of professionals listening to children and taking what they have to say seriously, but it is also about taking the child's views into account when drawing up the protection plan or deciding where they should be placed. Clearly some children, by virtue of age and understanding, are more able than others to participate in this process and it is important to note that the Act does not say that children's *wishes* are paramount. It may still be necessary to act in ways which do not accord with what they want but they have a right to be consulted, if not in open meetings then behind the scenes.

(d)   Previous good practice that child protection should be based on effective inter-agency liaison is reinforced both by the Act and by the Government guidance *Working Together* (see Appendix 2). This guide, together with local Area Child Protection Committee handbooks and procedures, is highly useful reading for all teaching staff and others with welfare or pastoral responsibilities within schools. A clear grasp of the teacher's role within such procedures is *essential*. This is not simply a question of preferred practice: it is a legal requirement that agencies must work together. The Act itself specifies various points in the investigation and protection process at which local authorities must consult LEAs. Such approaches must be responded to positively.

Governors' responsibilities

It is important not to assume that child protection issues arise only with respect to certain kinds of children in certain kinds of schools. Because much of this work is confidential, it is quite possible that, for example, governing bodies may not be aware that their staff are acting in this area. I recall an example of this when I was making a presentation about the Act to the governors of a primary school in a leafy suburb. When asked whether this was an issue for him, the headteacher replied that it was not so much the numbers of children involved as the amount of time required by each one for the job to be done properly. He then gave an estimate in double figures of the number of children who had been the subject of concern in the last two years. The shock wave which ran across the governors' faces was almost visible. Clearly few of them had any idea that such an issue might arise in their school!

This was a tribute not only to the headteacher's excellent record on confidentiality but also to the fact that governors do need to be given carefully managed information in order to be sure that they are in touch with the work of their staff. Otherwise they might not recognize the importance of their own responsibilities, not least the question of cost when supply teachers may be needed to cover staff absences at lengthy case conferences or when training and resources have to be bought in (see Appendix 1).

Implications of grant maintained status
There is a further important point in terms of where the responsibility lies now that schools not only manage their own budgets but may also be grant maintained by Whitehall rather than resourced by the LEA. *Working Together* para 4.36 makes it clear that schools which are not maintained by the LEA (which therefore includes both grant maintained schools and the independent sector) are the responsibility of the *Social Services Department* when it comes to making sure that staff and governors are aware of local procedures and carrying them out appropriately.

Governing bodies in these schools are expected to seek advice from their SSD and to ensure that proper procedures have been agreed. There may not be much noticeable change just yet but as the number of grant maintained schools grows, this will need careful handling to avoid the risk of schools being unaware of their duties. Eventually, issues such as who should represent grant maintained schools on Area Child Protection Committees and to whom they are accountable for their practice, will have to be addressed.

A typology of abuse

Child abuse may take many different forms and it pays for staff to be aware of the range of concerns which could become the subject of investigation. It is not just a question of unexplained injuries, though these would be a cause for concern. It may help to keep this wider typology in mind though these signs do not, of course, *prove* that the child is being abused:

- physical injury
  - bruises, scars, lacerations, burns
  - fractures or head injuries
  - internal pain, esp to abdomen or chest
- physical neglect
  - failure to thrive
  - inappropriate dressing (over- or underdressed)
  - hungry, dirty, tired, undernourished
- emotional injury
  - a suspicious, frightened child
  - emotional outbursts/uncontrolled behaviour
  - poor relationships with siblings/peers
- emotional neglect
  - an over-dependency on adults
  - slow development/delayed speech
  - a withdrawn, uncommunicative child
- sexual abuse (includes both unwanted/inappropriate sexual activity and exposure to sexual stimuli/pornography – may be boys as well as girls)
  - inappropriate sexual behaviour/ language
  - unusual shyness about changing/ showering
  - school avoidance/psychosomatic complaints/behavioural difficulties
- potential abuse
  - watch for the warning signs of a child trying to tell you something
  - be aware of any risk factors
  - keep relationships open and safe

The role of schools

What then are the general principles which now apply in defining the role of schools in protecting children? Although there may be some variation according to locally agreed procedures, *Working Together* makes it clear that the following criteria should be easily identifiable:

A school co-ordinator
There must be a designated senior member of staff in every school who is responsible for child protection matters. This should be a matter of LEA policy and it may not necessarily be the headteacher. LEAs are required to keep a list of who is responsible for child protection procedures in *every establishment which they maintain.* It may be that only this person makes any referrals, though this may be difficult in practice. They should at least see themselves as responsible for making sure that proper training has been given and that all staff, both teaching and non-teaching, are aware of the procedures to be followed. Procedural handbooks should not be kept under lock and key in the headteacher's office! Staff should all be familiar with the classic warning signs of a child at risk and feel confident of their role in responding. Governors should check that all of this is true for the school for which they carry ultimate responsibility.

Monitoring and referral
The education service does not constitute an investigation agency with respect to child protection, nor should school staff see it as their job to investigate allegations of criminal behaviour by either parents or children. Their primary tasks are monitoring and referral. These are extremely important tasks as studies have indicated that more children disclose the existence of abuse to school staff than to anyone else. This is entirely to be expected bearing in mind the amount of time which children spend at school and the extremely valuable nature of the relationships with teachers and others which are formed there.

But it also heightens the need to be sure that we understand the boundaries. It may mean having to 'let go' of a child about whom you feel very deeply and allowing someone else actually to steer him through the process of full disclosure. It is not normally appropriate for a child to have to tell his story over and over again. The task of the teacher will usually be to accumulate sufficient information to make a good quality referral, without going into the circumstances of the alleged abuse itself. Local procedures normally lay down that referral to the SSD, the Police or the NSPCC should immediately be confirmed in writing and recorded in the school's log-book. Appropriate LEA officers and medical personnel should also be informed.

If a referral is appropriate it will generally need to include:

- full details of the child's name, address, date of birth;
- details of other members of the household, siblings etc;

- details of all those with parental responsibility, including any such person who does not live with the child;
- whether there are any orders which relate to the child (eg, old custody orders or section 8 orders under the Children Act);
- name and telephone number of the child's GP;
- what the referrer has seen and heard;
- how they can be contacted again.

Confidentiality

It is *not* possible to give children an absolute guarantee that what they say will remain confidential. If they give real cause for concern, there is a duty to refer them to the appropriate authority. However, it is possible to make sure that the child understands who must be told about what. A teacher could, for example, promise that parents will not be informed without the child's knowledge but that he/she must tell a social worker anything that the child tells him/her. It should still be possible to create a climate of trust which helps a child to feel confident in disclosing but which enables appropriate action to be taken. With all but the youngest children, it is good practice to keep them fully informed about what is happening and what will be done with the information they give.

Even in situations where referral is not appropriate, teachers still have an important role to play in monitoring children's wellbeing and being sensitive to any signs of abuse. It should always be possible to discuss concerns with colleagues and others without fear that this will necessarily escalate the situation and lead to an over-reaction on the part of other agencies. Great care should be taken, however, to ensure the confidentiality of such consultation, especially within the school.

There is often more time than is sometimes thought in which to make a considered response rather than immediately rushing into irreversible procedures, though this does not mean that real causes for concern should be ignored. But it is important to recognize that the Children Act has dramatically changed the social work climate and there is no question nowadays of the child being 'whisked away' on the merest suspicion. If anything, teachers often feel some frustration at the apparent lack of urgency which may be displayed by child protection specialists. This should reflect a carefully managed process which is designed to steer a middle way between being over-zealous and too laissez-faire. If in doubt, talk to the local SSD Area Child Protection Team for advice.

Alleged abuse by staff

Procedures should exist to cover what happens if a member of the school staff is suspected or accused of abuse. This is a shared responsibility between the LEA and the governing body (in LEA maintained schools). It will place the headteacher in a difficult position in trying to balance responsibilities under disciplinary procedures and a duty to participate in formulating a plan to protect the child. These two strands to the issue, together with the third question of whether any criminal proceedings may become appropriate, will have to be carefully distinguished from each other. All governing bodies should feel entitled to guidance from the LEA or from the SSD as appropriate on how to formulate policy in this area. Teaching and non-teaching staff have a right to clear information about what these procedures are.

Child protection plans
School staff should be active participants in the drawing up of comprehensive assessments and plans for the future of a child who needs protection. Staff attending case conferences should be well informed and, wherever possible, able to supply the conference with written information of a clear and factual nature. Child protection conferences are not designed to establish the guilt or innocence of any particular person but they are a crucial part of inter-agency programmes to secure the on-going protection of the child. As a result of the shortened timetables which are a basic expectation of the Act at every level, there may be little time between initial investigation and the case conference. There is usually a quorum of agencies required and headteachers and governors should regard the attendance of key staff as a priority.

Registration
Proper procedures should be in place for making sure that schools are informed of the admission of children on to the child protection register, the content of their child protection plan and who is the responsible 'keyworker'. Clear arrangements should also exist for notification when a child's name is removed or for information concerning a child on the register to be moved confidentially between one school and another, eg, on secondary transfer.

These arrangements often operate through the education welfare/education social work service and should be applicable to all children in both LEA and grant maintained schools. Clearly there are important issues of information management here about which LEAs/governors should have clear policy. Such children should be carefully monitored and education staff have a right to be regarded as partners by fellow-professionals and so kept fully informed. On-going relationships with parents will be an important question to be clarified. Parents do not necessarily lose their rights under education law because their child has been admitted to the register or made the subject of a care order.

Curriculum issues

In addition to these statutory duties, teachers may also want to address issues of child protection through the curriculum. This may provide a forum for helping pupils to acquire skills in self-protection and enable them to take control over aspects of their lives which are causing them distress. Teaching staff should always be sensitive to the fact that any discussion of abuse, protection and risk may be the means by which a child is given sufficient confidence to disclose. A child who shows an unusual reluctance to participate may also be trying to tell us something and may need careful encouragement rather than any hint of criticism. There is a range of publications and resources available to assist in such classroom work.

Residential settings

Children in residential care of various kinds may have particular problems as they are separated from their parents and may not be easily able to communicate any problems which may arise, particularly if they have special needs. The general duty for promoting the welfare of children living away from home will normally lie with the SSD which has various responsibilities under the Children Act including the inspection and registration of children's homes and schools with boarding facilities (see p 54). Schools maintained by the LEA may be treated rather differently. After several scandals in recent years about the abuse of children in residential care, this is clearly an important issue.

Working Together contains clear guidance to cover the protection of children in residential schools. Policies and managerial procedures must recognize the possibility of abuse by either members of staff, other children or visitors and seek to prevent it. Clear, written procedures should exist which should ensure that issues which may arise are dealt with promptly and appropriately. When abuse is alleged against a fellow-resident both 'victim' and 'perpetrator' are entitled to protection and, if members of staff are suspected, an independent element within the process of investigation is essential.

It is important to ensure that children have an opportunity to voice any complaints which they might have about their treatment at the hands of staff or other residents. This is a difficult area and can be open to exploitation by children who are seeking to make trouble, but it would be extremely dangerous for staff and governors to assume that such allegations will always be without foundation. All children should be offered access to an independent means of complaint, either through a scheme of 'independent visitors', telephone helplines or clearly defined complaints procedures (see Chapter 5).

IMPLICATIONS OF THE 'WELFARE CHECKLIST'

The paramountcy principle

The welfare checklist in s1(3) of the Children Act is one of the most important parts of the legislation. It sets the tone for much of the emphasis on the welfare of the child as the 'paramount' consideration under the Act. There have been some examples of overstatement of the application of this section, in that the Act does define certain circumstances in which the checklist *must* be applied whereas in other circumstances it may be set aside. But delivering the welfare of children is the Act's central concern and this list of areas is crucial to understanding its approach. The inclusion of 'educational needs' in s1(3)(b) as one of the required factors to which consideration must be given is therefore of considerable significance, not least to those who are responsible for trying to meet them!

Educational needs

It is, of course, good news that the checklist recognizes that a child's educational needs are integral to his welfare. Educational professionals do not always feel that other agencies acknowledge the importance of education and this has also been true of some courts in the past. The Children Act's approach is to treat children as 'whole', accepting that one part of their lives cannot be isolated and dealt with without considering the relationship between that area and others. If a child is to be made the subject of a care order, how will he be educated? If a child's father is to be granted a residence order to enable the child to live with him following a divorce, where will he go to school? The whole principle of the Act is that orders should not be made at all unless they can be demonstrated to be of positive benefit to the child. How *can* that be demonstrated if issues as significant as education are not to be sorted out till afterwards?

The checklist sets education in a context; within the child's range of needs, physical, emotional and educational. This gives support to models of learning which do not seek to isolate education from everything else but which recognize that children need to be understood in the light of their total circumstances, personal and social, physical and intellectual. This is reflected also in the Act's broad definition of 'development' in s17 which defines a wide range of aspects of a child's life where issues of 'significant harm' may arise.

Here is useful evidence for embracing the Children Act as powerful ammunition in ensuring that 'education' is understood in its broadest sense and that children's needs are recognized within the school community in the light of the contexts from which they come. The checklist allows a wide interpretation of significant factors, including any racial, linguistic, cultural or religious aspects of a child's identity and expects people making decisions about their lives to take all these factors into account.

Assisting the court

Section 1(3) applies whenever care or supervision orders are being sought and in private proceedings where there is a contested issue to be decided. It means, in practice, that courts should consult with schools *before* making important decisions about a child in order to establish the significance of the decision for their educational needs. Schools should be prepared to consult with court welfare officers and local authority social workers who are assisting the court by drawing up reports. School staff may have something unique to say which can enable the court to make an informed decision and they should be given the opportunity to say it. They may also be able to help the court with other aspects of the welfare checklist, such as the likely effect on the child of any changes in his circumstances especially if their experience of the child and his family goes back over several years.

However, there is another side to this coin as, in common with other areas of the Act, with opportunity comes responsibility. School staff may feel nervous about committing themselves, especially where the capabilities of parents are concerned or about which of the parents seems better suited to appreciate the child's needs. The spirit of openness which pervades all Children Act proceedings, in which reports and information are shared with all parties including the child, may make staff nervous in case they offend parents with whom they may have to go on working. This demands considerable skill and staff should not be expected to handle such responsibilities without adequate support and training.

Education welfare officers/social workers (EWOs/ESWs) will be key allies in assisting with this process but they may not be able to provide the appropriate information themselves. The bottom line must always be that the teacher is acting in what they consider to be the best welfare interests of the child, even if this means having to make difficult judgements. Such judgements must, however, be based on fact and not merely on stereotypes or speculation. The growing movement towards standardized assessments should help in the giving of objective and factual information about a child's educational progress and how this relates to the provision which he needs.

Accountability

There is one further implication of the welfare checklist. The inclusion of 'educational needs' introduces an element of external scrutiny into how those needs are being met which may sometimes prove uncomfortable. The court's concern is not only what a child's needs are but also whether they are being met in a way which ensures his welfare – the paramount consideration. Let us say that a child is the subject of family proceedings because his parents are disputing where he should live. In the course of its enquiries the court establishes that the child has a serious problem with absence from school, or has been permanently excluded and no other school has been found, or appears to have special educational needs which the parents claim are not being met.

This now ceases to be a matter between the LEA/school and the family and becomes an issue for the court to clarify. The court may ask questions about what has been done to address these problems: has the family been offered help by the education welfare service, why was the child excluded, what special needs assessment has been made? Courts may become the point at which the buck stops in their role as the ultimate guardian of the child's welfare. Decisions made by school staff and others may have to be accounted for later when the question of how the child's educational needs have been met is being reviewed by the court. Well-documented decisions, made with proper reflection and consultation with both parents and children and which have had as their focus the perceived best interests of the child, will be the best basis from which to respond to such enquiries.

THE WELFARE OF CHILDREN AT SCHOOL

Education welfare services

In addition to this specific use of the welfare checklist in court situations, the Act creates a new incentive for schools to address the general issue of children's welfare and how this is safeguarded and promoted within the educational process. Children spend an enormous amount of their time at school, in a context which many, including the Government, would see as an essential part of society's responsibility for ensuring their wellbeing and proper development. Children do not learn if they are unhappy or distressed by what is happening in their families, or if the circumstances of their lives outside school are constantly undermining the efforts of their teachers. Schools are reflections of the communities which they serve and when communities are under pressure from poverty, poor housing or unemployment this inevitably has a knock-on effect.

This has been recognized for over 100 years by the provision of LEA-funded education welfare officers or education social workers who have a wide range of responsibilities for promoting the welfare of children in the school setting. This will primarily involve working with children who have difficulty with attendance (see Chapter 4), through to administering national benefits such as free school meals or discretionary schemes to assist with the costs of school clothing. Much home–school liaison is undertaken by these officers, who have increasingly become better qualified and more equipped to handle the complexities of modern family life. Most EWOs/ESWs have duties under child protection procedures and assist in the support given to children with special educational needs. They also have responsibility for ensuring that the welfare of children is safeguarded outside their lives at school, for example, the registration and monitoring of child employment or working with excluded pupils.

These services are set to continue as part of the 'mandatory exception', *whether or not the school becomes grant maintained*, albeit in a changed context in the light of the reform of school management and financing. The statutory welfare responsibility remains with the LEA for *all* children in state schools. But clearly it cannot be delivered without the active participation of teaching and tutorial staff and, as schools gain greater control over their own resources, it is likely that new ways will emerge in which these tasks can be addressed. There are fewer than 3,000 EWOs/ESWs for a school population of 8.5 million. New partnerships will be necessary and it is essential that school managers and teachers are confident of their role in the delivery of pupil welfare. Three areas in particular are relevant in the light of the Children Act's principle of paramountcy for the welfare of children: pastoral care, equality of opportunity and assisting children in need.

Pastoral care

A commitment to quality

All schools seek to exercise some kind of pastoral care towards their pupils, either informally or through well-managed responses which may involve specialist staff freed from other duties. One of the more worrying consequences of the pressure on school budgets in recent years has been the temptation to see such provision as an extra which can be set aside in favour of what 'must' be done. There is certainly little or no public recognition for the efforts which a school makes in this direction.

But in these days of parental choice it does not seem unreasonable that one of the areas which a school may want to stress as a performance indicator is the quality of its pastoral care. Statements in school brochures can provide an opportunity to go beyond generalized good intentions into specific indications of the way in which the school manages its care of pupils and the resources it gives to implementing it. *All* children will need this kind of care at some point, not only those whose lives are permanently in a state of uncertainty or those experiencing acute crisis. Any parent may wish to see that this responsibility is recognized and affirmed.

Sadly, pastoral care sometimes becomes identified with disciplinary procedures which not only confuses children and parents but also places the teacher in an impossible position if they are called on to be a caring figure one moment and the dispenser of sanctions the next. The emphasis in the Children Act on the needs of the whole child should be reflected in a range of expertise being available which can be used appropriately according to the needs of the individual.

Ideally this should include counsellors and people skilled in working with groups. In my experience at least, teachers are often asked to carry out these tasks with little training and even less support. Children bring all kinds of problems to school with them, increasingly so, and pastoral staff are frequently required to demonstrate their skills within inter-agency contexts where expectations of professionalism will be high.

Schools are in danger of being by-passed in the delivery of children's welfare if managers and headteachers do not recognize that this is as important and specialized a skill as teaching itself. This has been reflected to some extent in the training on the Children Act given to other agencies. Schools have not always been recognized as caring communities in the way that they deserve and the welfare aspect of educational provision is often the subject of misunderstanding and criticism. Perhaps one of the most useful ways of addressing this is by ensuring that approaches to caring for children's needs are as inter-agency based as possible, drawing on the expertise of other professionals as appropriate. Membership of national organizations such as the National Association for Pastoral Care in Education may also be an indicator of whether there is a genuine commitment to high standards in this area.

Bullying and bullies
One key area in the delivery of good pastoral care to children is undoubtedly a policy to combat bullying. Schools are often large communities, sometimes reflecting an age range which includes virtual adults as well as those not yet physically or emotionally mature. There are plenty of opportunities for violence and intimidation and, as with child protection, no school should feel it is exempt from the need to address the issues in a formal and open way. Some studies have suggested that almost half of the children interviewed had experienced bullying in one form or another. Parents are entitled to know that all reasonable measures have been taken to ensure the safety of their children at school. Children are entitled to reassurances that their fears and complaints will be taken seriously, even if the bullying is from a teacher or if the culture of the school emphasizes physical toughness.

'Childline' received over 5,000 calls about the problems of bullying in 1992 and there have been several well-publicized suicides where it has appeared to be a factor. There are strict standards applying to the wellbeing of children in residential settings and rightly so. But much of the violence against children happens in minor and occasionally serious ways at ordinary schools. No system or strategy can be foolproof but any school which claims to have the welfare of its pupils at heart should surely have a clear strategy both for preventing and dealing with bullying, ideally one which has involved the pupils directly in drawing it up and carrying it out.

In this context it is important to remember that the bully will also be a child in trouble who needs pastoral care in his own right. This is a difficult double responsibility for schools to handle and, quite reasonably, children whose behaviour is unacceptable need to be disciplined and sometimes even excluded. No policy on bullying can simply excuse the bully. However, there is some evidence that this process of labelling certain children as unmanageable or violent can become rather arbitrary and, of course, any child who manifests such behaviour needs *his* problems addressing too, albeit sometimes away from the mainstream school environment.

There will be few prizes for the school which tries to meet the needs of difficult children but there are growing signs that society will not tolerate them simply being thrown out of the system to cause even greater havoc elsewhere. Alternative educational provision will be difficult to resource in the current climate and, despite newly proposed initiatives in this area, many off-site special units have been under threat with the ever-increasing emphasis on devolving as much of the finance to schools as possible. (Some system whereby the money follows the child is surely essential, as provided for in a late amendment to the 1993 Education Act.)

Schools will still be expected to cope in all but the most extreme of cases and so will need positive strategies for doing so. The Elton Report on disruptive behaviour in schools still repays much study in this context and many LEAs have been preparing guidance on the management of such pupils in response. The welfare of *every* child is paramount, even those who are angry and disturbed. We must have an education system which meets the needs of all children. This is clearly difficult to reconcile with other expectations being placed on schools in terms of performance etc and teachers should be able to call upon a range of services to support them. Most of all, they will want recognition from the Government of the personal commitment involved in befriending those whom others might not consider worth the bother. Bricks cannot be made without straw!

Equal opportunities

Anti-racist practice
Schools should also be communities which reflect the equal opportunities aspects of the Children Act. All schools should have positive policies in place which actively seek to promote cultural understanding and combat racism and discrimination. There are specific points in the Children Act at which local authorities are under a duty to ensure that they have taken account of the child's racial, linguistic, cultural and religious identity. The welfare checklist, while not specifically mentioning it, has been widely seen as affirming the importance of these aspects of a child's background and circumstances. Children's welfare is clearly best promoted by recognizing the importance of such issues where applicable. Children are entitled to have their religious and cultural traditions respected and good practice in schools will surely serve society well for the future.

But there has also been some suspicion among ethnic minority communities about the Act. This has not been helped by the fact that the DoH (unlike the DfE) publishes no information leaflets about its provisions in minority languages. The general purposes of the Act have been interpreted by some as designed to address the problems of the white community – child protection, unruly children, divorce etc. This is clearly an over-simplification, but there have certainly been examples of tension when professionals have tried to apply the Act impartially. This may be particularly true in schools which now find themselves required to ensure that their religious and moral context is 'broadly Christian' at the same time as trying to respect and work with other traditions and beliefs.

As will be seen in the next chapter, the Act's basic concepts of the family are still very Western in tone, with a clear emphasis on the authority of natural parents. There is a recognition that 'family' should be interpreted widely but there may still be difficulty with respect to cultures where the extended family is the norm and networks of authority may be very different. The extent to which the wishes and feelings of children about their own welfare will be respected within their families and community also varies greatly. Yet schools must apply the same expectations to all children and this may require careful thinking to ensure that a proper balance is being struck in pastoral practice between the various rights and responsibilities involved.

Special educational needs
There are similar issues with respect to special educational needs and children with disabilities and learning difficulties. One of the most welcome things about the Act, and the consequent reorganisations in SSDs which it has encouraged, is the insistence that children with disabilities are children first and disabled second. The 1993 Education Act affirms that the proper place for children with special educational needs is within the mainstream provision made for all other children, unless their needs specifically require otherwise. Schools will want to be affirming in their acceptance of children with special needs by ensuring that buildings are accessible and that any other, less physical, obstacles are overcome.

But there are contrary forces operating here as well; the difficulty in obtaining sufficient resources at the local school level to make this vision a reality; the feelings of some parents that they prefer 'special' schools for their children (or other people's!) and the range of special needs which a school may have to try and accommodate within its life. Inevitably there are 'deserving' and 'undeserving' criteria in many people's minds which may lead to equal opportunities for the child from an academically gifted background who is wheelchair-bound with muscular dystrophy but rather less enthusiasm for the child from a family of travellers whose attendance is erratic but who has significant problems with reading and needs just as much extra help to manage the school day.

These issues should, wherever possible, be the subject of properly thought-out policy by school managers, not just dependent on the perceptions and commitment of individual members of staff. No school will have 'children from minority groups unwelcome' in its brochure but some may send that signal unless their emphasis on children's welfare is explicit and consistent. The Children Act provides an excellent opportunity to formulate such a policy if none exists already.

'Children in need'

Family services

Schools will also have a significant contribution to make in assisting children 'in need'. Children who are in need of services from the local authority (defined in s17) are a special focus of the Act and their parents are entitled to assistance in bringing them up effectively. Many parents need extra help with their children, either because of their own lack of confidence or skills, or because the children themselves pose extra demands through disabilities and behaviour, or because the environment in which the parents have to operate is one of poverty, homelessness and particular stress. This is about much more than children with special *educational* needs (though most local authorities will include such children within their overall definition). The primary responsibility will be towards children who need protection, but children 'in need' is a much wider concept and a considerable number of individuals in some schools could be included.

The range of services which should be available is set out in Schedule 2 Part I of the Act. It includes provision for children with disabilities, action to prevent the need for supervision, care or criminal proceedings, advice, guidance, counselling and family centres etc. Under s27 the local authority may call on other agencies to assist as required in making these services available to those who require them. No adverse judgement is intended; it is purely a question of needs.

Parents and children naturally look to schools for help when they are experiencing difficulty, probably long before most of them think of approaching the SSD. For many it is the most local, user-friendly service available; the place to go to when a problem arises. Many schools are extremely adept at managing such a role – pastoral care for parents as much as for children – and some have deliberately set out to be seen as a resource for the whole community.

Schools may have valuable premises which can be made available for after-school clubs or holiday playschemes (specifically referred to in s18(5)), run either in partnership with other agencies such as the Youth and Community Service, or by volunteer groups and community associations. Some schools offer spare classroom space for mother-and-toddler groups or actively involve the pupils in community work with children and families. The Children Act should provide a new focus for resourcing such projects as s17(5) places a specific duty on local authorities to facilitate such provision by others as well as resourcing it itself.

'Accommodated' children

It is important to mention in this context the changed circumstances of children who may need to live away from their parents because of problems within their family or because they take a lot of looking after at home. One of the services which a local authority must make available for children in need is 'accommodation' under s20. The SSD may make arrangements for a child to be looked after by foster-carers or in a residential unit, at the request of their parents. This may be for a short or longer period; it may be a regular arrangement from time to time or just a 'one off'. No court proceedings are involved and no inference should be made about the parents or the quality of their caring – they have the right to such help in bringing up their children.

The old concept of 'voluntary care' is no longer applicable to such situations as the child is *not* 'in care' (although this language is still used, even by some social workers). In the past voluntary care could become a care order by the back door but this can no longer happen. No notice is required for parents to have the children back home again and all the parental responsibility remains with them. Social workers should liaise with schools about the arrangements if applicable. An agreement should be drawn up detailing who is responsible for what during the period of accommodation and schools have a right to know what the effects of these arrangements are. Parents' continued involvement with their children at school should be encouraged wherever reasonable. (There is a duty to make every effort to accommodate the child near to where they live so that they can carry on their life as normally as possible.)

Breaking down the barriers

This is the part of the Act which probably has most implications for resources, and which will not become reality unless there is a real commitment to making it happen. The whole preventive tone of this section requires a level of services which few local authorities can afford in the current financial climate in local government. Many children in need whose families might benefit from the provision of accommodation will not receive such help because there are no appropriate placements available. Joint-funding projects such as day centres and support schemes are under continuous threat as money is concentrated on the statutory services which are considered most urgent, such as child protection.

But many teachers and EWOs/ESWs would affirm that such acute services fail to address the needs of those children who, if their families were helped now, might not reach the point where crisis intervention is needed. That *should* be one of the primary changes brought about by the Act. Teachers are usually in the front line of trying to meet the needs of such children, often feeling that other agencies are not interested until disaster strikes. These sections of the Children Act are essential information for all those seeking to develop their role as partners in caring and looking for a lobbying point to assist them.

The Children Act's vision of a network of co-operative agencies working together to help children in need and their parents will strike many educational professionals as an impossible ideal. There has been more money to implement the Act – a lot more money – but schools have rarely been given the opportunity to share in its distribution and allocation. There is still an urgent need for us to break out of our tightly defined boundaries so that the needs of the whole child may be addressed in a more corporate way. A few councils are beginning to experiment with LEA/SSD mergers. There are those who predict some kind of 'Ministry for Children' involving all those services aimed at children from within Social Services, Health and Education. With the moves towards the separation of services for adults and children within SSDs and the reducing role of the LEA, that may well be the natural direction to be followed if the Children Act is pursued to its logical conclusion.

There is provision within the Schedules for assessments to be made on an inter-agency basis to avoid the possibility of, say, an educational assessment being made six months after a health assessment and a social work assessment six months after that. No professional should feel in total control of their own contribution as there may be times when the timetables of other agencies need to take priority so that a child's needs can be properly met. How would teachers react if the educational psychologist could not pick up the child of greatest concern because they are responding to a request from another agency about another child who needs assessment now? How would such breaking down of barriers relate to feelings of professional competence and specialized knowledge? How could a unified service ever become a reality if the DoH and the DfE appear to be unaware of each other's legislation? Teachers and governors, and indeed parents, are caught in a web of conflicting expectations. There is still a real danger that the welfare of children in need will sometimes slip through altogether.

INDEPENDENT BOARDING SCHOOLS

A special responsibility

While the bulk of the guidance in this book is addressed to the needs of children in day-schools, both LEA and grant maintained (and, as a matter of good practice, independent day schools), there are specific requirements in the Children Act for certain independent schools with boarding facilities. Monitoring these establishments does not, by and large, fall to the LEA but to the SSD, and such schools should already have established procedures for implementing the various regulations. As with other areas concerning outside inspections under the Act, these provisions have proved to be a focus of some dispute and expectations are constantly being revised. However, this brief summary may serve as a guide to the general issues involved in this context, alongside the issues which need to be addressed by all schools. It should not, however, be thought that this is the *only* section of relevance to independent schools.

The key part of the Act is s87 which places a duty on the proprietors of certain residential schools to 'safeguard and promote' the welfare of children within them. As was noted with child protection, children living away from their parents may be in particular need of procedures which ensure that they are not being exposed to unreasonable risks or threats to their wellbeing. The Act has made it clear that the best way of making sure that such children are well cared for lies in closer arrangements for monitoring and inspection of what might otherwise become a rather 'closed' part of a child's life. The accompanying guidance to the Act (Volume 5) is essential reading for all those who may have duties in this area. The inspection procedure is set out in the Inspection of Premises, Children and Records (Independent Schools) Regulations 1991, which arise from s87(6) and are included in an Annex to Volume 5.

The scope of the Act

Certain kinds of residential schools do not come within the scope of s87. In general these are:

- Independent schools which have fewer than 51 children in residence, and which are *not* approved under the 1981 Education Act to educate children subject to a statement of special educational needs. The requirement on these schools to register as 'children's homes' was removed by s292 Education Act 1993 from January 1994.
- Schools as above which are required to register under Part I of the Registered Homes Act 1984. (These provide residential care for children with physical disabilities or mental disorders and are already subject to registration and monitoring arrangements.)
- 'Special schools' which are already subject to inspection. However, any LEA or health authority which accommodates a child for more than three months continuously must inform the SSD of the area in which that child is 'ordinarily resident', so that they can ensure the child's welfare is being adequately safeguarded. This will not normally include any special school in which children go home for the holidays. Children given year-round care may be subject to the private fostering regulations under Part IX.

Promoting a child's welfare has to do with the 'health, happiness and proper physical, intellectual, emotional, social and behavioural development of that child, as well as protecting him against the risk of suffering significant harm or neglect' (para 2.4.1). It is recognized that a very wide range of children may be being cared for within independent schools and that arrangements might need to be very different for the older child who maintains regular contact with his parents than for the younger child whose parents are abroad or are separated from him for a prolonged period.

It has to be remembered that for many parents undergoing family breakdown, residential education is a preferred option in order to ensure that some stability is retained in the child's life or when neither parent may be able to offer him a permanent home. (The guidance in Chapter 3 of this book about parental responsibility may be of particular significance in this context and independent schools should recognize their obligations towards both parents wherever appropriate.)

Good practice in this area will be a combination of the insights and skills to be found within both residential education and child care social work. It is important to establish dialogue and mutual understanding between the two fields so that each may be informed by the insights of the other. This has not always happened very successfully. Although it is the responsibility of the SSD to do the inspecting, this should not mean that experience arising from educational practice should be ignored. There is much good practice within the independent sector already. However, the focus of these arrangements is not the quality of the *educational* provision and proprietors will need to accept that the observations of other professionals may need to be given proper consideration when it comes to children's wider needs.

Inspecting children's welfare

The guidance sets out a list of areas where attention may need to be given to the welfare of children. It provides, incidentally, a useful checklist for any school – even allowing for omitting the sections on the quality of the accommodation and outside contacts.

(a) *Management* – the ultimate responsibility for all these issues lies with the school's proprietors and managers to ensure that policy and procedures are in place which protect children's welfare. This ranges from appropriate staff/student ratios to statements of policy in brochures etc. There should be written statements of good practice and effective arrangements for ensuring that they are carried out.

(b) *Child protection* – as with all educational establishments, both teaching and non-teaching staff must be alert to the needs of children at any particular risk and confident of their own knowledge of locally agreed procedures. The specific responsibilities of the SSD with respect to independent schools mean that any concerns raised in the course of such monitoring should automatically lead to investigation if this is required.

(c) *Staff recruitment* – proprietors must take great care in checking the calibre and history of all those members of staff given the responsibility of caring for other people's children, especially those placed in positions of trust. Temporary workers and volunteers will also require careful monitoring to ensure that children are being adequately cared for. They should not be expected to undertake duties for which they have not been properly trained or during which they are not adequately supervised. 'List 99' from the DfE (a confidential list of those unsuitable for employment in schools) and the DoH's consultancy service should be used accordingly. It will be part of the inspection responsibility of the SSD to ensure that such procedures have been properly carried out.

(d) *Accommodation* – there are many popular misconceptions of boarding schools, probably arising mostly from our childhood reading. The Education (School Premises) Regulations 1981 represent a rather more thorough approach to children's needs by recognizing that children require their own 'personal space' while gaining the benefits of living in a community. A combination of opportunities for privacy with experience of living as a group should be available as the basis of an effective caring environment.

(e) *Health* – children require regular monitoring of their health as an essential indicator of their welfare. The guidance underlines the importance of enabling particularly older children to have some say in who is responsible for their health care. A doctor of the same sex may be of particular significance for some pupils, as might entirely confidential treatment when required. This area could be a responsibility which weighs particularly heavily on some schools, especially where the parents are not readily accessible. Issues of diet, hygiene, lifestyle and personal relationships should be attended to and clear procedures must exist for dealing with serious accidents, illnesses and even deaths.

(f) *Safety* – the recent canoeing accident involving pupils from a Plymouth school has reminded all schools of the importance of safety when caring for other people's children. In residential settings there should be regular fire drills at various times, including during the night, together with appropriate inspections of buildings and facilities. Children should receive all reasonable supervision and attention to any potential risks. Proprietors are responsible for ensuring that all necessary procedures are known to, and carried out by, the whole school community. (Particular attention should be paid to issues of parental delegation of authority in this context, as outlined in Chapter 3.)

(g) *Outside contacts* – in the post-'pindown' environment reflected by the Children Act, attention to children's contacts outside the establishment has become particularly important. Children are entitled to private facilities for both meeting visitors and telephoning parents and others. Children's mail is also private – specifically referred to in the UN

Convention on the Rights of the Child. Intriguingly, the guidance refers to the need 'with older children' for staff sometimes to be aware of the contents of letters and that 'this should be achieved by the children opening mail in front of staff' (para 3.7). This seems rather strange. There is also a comment about obtaining parental consent for staff to open mail addressed to younger children, 'for example, where parents are separated'. Bearing in mind the right of anyone with parental responsibility to act independently of anyone else with parental responsibility, unless there are orders restricting their actions, this advice seems of dubious validity and great caution should be exercised here. There would have to be real grounds for believing that a child's welfare was at risk to justify such actions. The consent of the person writing the letter would surely be required, not simply the permission of another parent or a third party.

(h) *Religion/culture* – the Children Act recognizes the significance of a child's religious, cultural, racial and linguistic background and beliefs and that children are entitled to adequate opportunity to give expression to them. School managers should expect to have policy statements in brochures as well as equal opportunities practices which ensure that they are carried out.

(i) *Personal relations and discipline* – those with the care of children are empowered by s3(5) of the Act to do what is reasonable to promote and safeguard their welfare, subject to the authority of those who have parental responsibility for them. This is a particularly important empowerment in a residential context and here too school staff will want to be sure that proper delegation has taken place by those who actually have the legal authority to do it. The quality of relationships within the school, both among pupils and between pupils and staff, should create an environment of mutual respect and co-operation. Children themselves should be a part of decision-making in this area and expectations about behaviour and discipline should be clear and consistent in practice. Such policy must be available both to parents and to the SSD. The comprehensive (though not all-embracing) restriction on the use of corporal punishment is relevant here and the guidance reminds proprietors and SSDs to be aware of the implications. Para 3.9.5 sets out the strict criteria which must be observed in the very limited circumstances where corporal punishment may still be administered in the independent sector. (This has proved a somewhat controversial area, with some SSD inspectors seeking to outlaw all such punishment. S293 Education Act now states that any such punishment must not be 'inhuman or degrading.'

(j) *Restricting liberty* – this is not likely to be appropriate in any residential independent school but s25 of the Act sets out the legal framework under which children looked after by a local authority can have their liberty restricted. Para 3.10.3 of the guidance warns proprietors that in the absence of specific legal authority, imposing any such restriction may render them liable to civil action.

(k) *Complaints* – as will be seen in Chapter 5, children should have opportunities to complain if they feel they are being treated unfairly or unreasonably. This process should include access to persons independent of the establishment. This is especially important in this context.

Procedures

Section 87(5) of the Children Act empowers the SSD (through an 'authorized person'), to enter any school covered by this section at any reasonable time. All independent schools should have had at least one formal inspection. Most should now be receiving at least a second visit to 'ensure that all the guidance contained in this Volume has been implemented'. There is no prescribed frequency with which inspections should take place thereafter, however inspection every two years with a more limited annual visit in between is anticipated in the guidance. Visits should normally be notified in advance. Written reports should be prepared and the Department's views concerning the welfare of the children recorded. These are not usually published, but they should be shown to the school in draft form so that any errors can be corrected. A final copy of the report must go to the school and to the DfE or the Welsh Office as appropriate.

If the SSD has serious concerns about the welfare of the children in the school, s87(4) requires it to notify the Secretary of State, (the 'Notice of Complaint'), having first discussed its concerns with the appropriate officials. There is provision for schools ultimately to be removed from the Register of Independent Schools if satisfactory outcomes are not forthcoming. Schools have a right of appeal to an Independent Schools Tribunal and clear grounds must be specified by the SSD if such action is taken.

Children placed in independent schools by local authorities or by LEAs continue to be the responsibility of such placing agencies under other regulations, in addition to those applying under the Children Act.

3

Parents, Schools and the Children Act

PARENTAL RESPONSIBILITY

A new model of parenthood

While the Children Act's primary aim is to promote the welfare of children, it has to be understood that its preferred way of doing it is through the promotion of parenthood. If the philosophical starting point is that 'parents know best', then it becomes the task of the rest of us to encourage and support them in acting effectively for the ultimate benefit of their children. The intervention of any agency in the life of a family should be on this basis.

Parents are to be taken seriously as part of the answer rather than being dismissed too readily as the cause of the problem. This emphasis, together with the changes made to the private law, particularly with regard to the position of parents who do not live with their children following a divorce or separation, has led some to conclude that the Act is more of another 'Parent's Charter' rather than the 'Children's Charter' which is sometimes claimed.

It is undoubtedly true that the Act does offer a new approach to parenthood and the status of parents is much enhanced, especially biological parents. But it would be a mistake to see this only in terms of 'rights'. The Act's chosen word is 'responsibility' and this is a vital clue to all that follows. Laws do not make people good parents; but they can set a climate which fosters positive and creative attitudes. Although there may yet be legislation which makes divorce more difficult, including the possibility of a compulsory cooling-off period before a decree is granted, this is not the concern of the Children Act. Accepting that we live in a society where many changes are taking place in family life and when established concepts about marriage etc are being questioned, how can the welfare of children best be secured in a way which supports their parents and helps them still act effectively?

Exercising parental responsibility
The definition of parental responsibility provides the answer: 'all the rights, duties, powers, responsibilities and authority which by law a parent has in relation to the child and his property' (s3(1)).

This is a rounded concept in contrast to what was seen as an excessive emphasis on rights in the past. When a child went into the care of the local authority before the Children Act, the authority 'assumed parental rights'. That was what it got from the parent and which now made it the parent instead. The emphasis now, however, is on the parental relationship existing for the benefit of the child rather than for the benefit of the parent. Parents *are* given more rights and authority in determining what will happen to their children, but they are also expected to act in ways which use that authority to promote the child's welfare rather than their own. Only when this is palpably not the case do authorities have a duty to ask courts to intervene.

There is no area of a child's life in which the exercise of responsible parenthood is more important than their education. Not only does this process last for 11 or more years but, as has already been noted, recent legislation has dramatically increased the available opportunities for parents to influence what goes on at school. Twenty years ago it might have been possible for the reforms of the Children Act to pass schools by with very little impact. Parents were often shadowy figures who were required for little more than the occasional parents' evening and the Christmas concert.

The whole climate is now radically different. There is a statutory requirement on school governing bodies that parents must be offered a whole range of information and given opportunities to respond to it. Parental choice is at the heart of the entire system and parents are rightly demanding much greater say in what happens to their own children at school. Of course, not all parents choose to take advantage of these rights, but they must be offered without discrimination. It is not acceptable for schools to do the choosing over which parents to involve; that must rest with the parents themselves in so far as that is possible in their particular circumstances.

The essential question

This is why it has become essential that school staff are able to answer one crucial question with respect to every child – *'Who has parental responsibility for this child?'* This has become the fundamental starting point on admission, and at every point where an important issue has arisen with respect to a child's education. Even though remarkably few books about pastoral care seem to recognize the fact, it cannot be assumed that the answer must be the two people living at home with him. 'Home–school liaison' is not sufficient to cover all the possibilities. That simply flies in the face of the reality of family life for millions of children. How can a school offer effective involvement to *all* its parents if staff do not even know both who those parents are *and* where they live? Without such information, how can headteachers and governors be confident that people who have every right to be involved have not been ignored?

It is people with parental responsibility who have the legal authority with respect to *their* child; they are the decision-makers who must be consulted. Any authority which the school has is derived from them. It is extremely poor practice if they only find out later what other people have already decided, yet this will be a frequent occurrence unless schools take the Children Act seriously. Important mistakes will be made which could lead ultimately to the making of court orders to prohibit certain actions which the school has unwittingly allowed. Decisions which have been made may have to be reversed with consequent embarrassment all round. If ignorance of the law cannot be held to be an excuse there is much learning to be done.

The beauty of the Children Act is that it is entirely logical and consistent – though some would say not always fair –in establishing who has parental responsibility for any child. It is not difficult to determine in most cases, but it does require a willingness on all sides to be open and honest in giving and receiving the information. It is this reluctance to share the facts, and the reluctance of schools to ask for them, which cause the biggest problem. Coping with the data will raise many complicated questions, but the concept itself is relatively simple and easily explained (see figure 3.1).

Married parents
People who are married each have parental responsibility for any child of that marriage, provided they are the biological mother and father. They hold it equally, permanently and each can act independently of the other in exercising it. They do not need each other's permission to make most decisions about the child, but, as each has an equal right to make them, they should both be consulted wherever possible by any relevant agency. There is therefore no longer

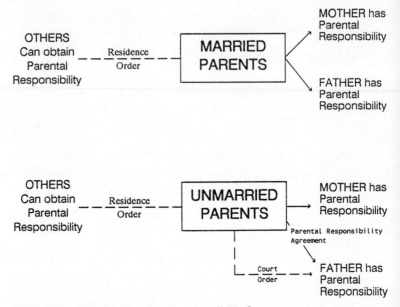

Figure 3.1 *Who has parental responsibility?*

any sense, as there was prior to the Children Act, that the father is the legal guardian of a legitimate child and carries the ultimate authority. Of course, when there is more than one person with parental responsibility, and they disagree with each other about the child, the decision of one or the other will have to be accepted. But either one of them could make the decision and there is no hierarchy which will enable an automatic preference for one or the other.

Parents in dispute
In the event of dispute, school staff have to decide which parent they believe to be acting in the child's best interests. This may be best established by asking the child, though even this need not be decisive. The aggrieved parent then has recourse through the courts if they feel sufficiently strongly about the issue (see section 8 orders, p 71). In many situations it might be best not to make any significant changes to the child's situation (for example a change of name by which they are known, when no actual legal change has been made), unless *all* those with parental responsibility are in agreement. There is a need to balance parents' independent rights against the concept of pro-ceeding by agreement wherever possible. This is often a difficult balance to strike and can probably only be learnt by experience rather than be defined on paper. (It sometimes helps to look at the decision

from the perspective of the person who is 'losing'. If you would not want that to happen to you, is it the right thing to do?)

Divorced/separated parents
This situation of shared responsibility is entirely unaffected by what happens to the relationship between the parents. *Only adoption removes their parental responsibility.* The parents may separate, divorce or remarry; the child may live with only one of them or neither of them; whatever happens in the future, if people have parental responsibility by virtue of ever having been married, they always have it until their child is 18, unless he is adopted by someone else. They should therefore each continue to be consulted about the child's education and offered all the rights of a parent in exactly the same way as before. Not living with the child or being divorced from the child's other parent in no way ends their responsibility.

These changes are retrospective; ie, anyone who was ever married in the past now has parental responsibility for any children of that marriage, even if they are now divorced and only one parent was given 'custody, care and control' at the time (Schedule 14.6). The custody arrangements still stand but they determine only where the child must live and which parent should have care of them day to day. Anyone else with parental responsibility is free to exercise it, provided they do not break the custody conditions.

So, for example, the parent who is living with the child cannot act as if they were the only person with any responsibility, if the child's other parent, to whom they were once married, is still alive. Although they will normally make routine decisions, especially if there is an order saying that the child should live with them, this does not give them the right to deny their former spouse the opportunity to exercise *their* parental responsibility, provided this does not infringe any order.

It should therefore be commonplace for two parents, no longer married but each with parental responsibility, to make independent arrangements with their child's school about how they will each continue to be offered their rights and opportunities as a parent. It is not possible for one parent to ask a school to deny their present or former spouse reasonable involvement in their own child's education, no matter how much their own relationship has been damaged. Only a court can order such restrictions. (All of this applies only to those biological parents who are, or have been, married.)

Unmarried parents
Where parents are unmarried, *only* the mother has parental

responsibility, unless the father has obtained it. If he is appointed a guardian (see p 70), or if he marries the mother, he obtains parental responsibility as a consequence, but he may obtain it in one of two other ways while remaining unmarried:

(a) by obtaining a parental responsibility order from the court. These are made on application through 'family proceedings' in either a magistrates' or a county court. Any unmarried father wishing to seek such an order should be advised to see a solicitor. The order remains in force until discharged by the court and may be made even if the mother is not willing, if the court feels that this is in the best interests of the child;

(b) much more commonly, an unmarried father can obtain parental responsibility by agreement with the mother where she is willing to share it with him. (They do not have to be living together.) This agreement *must* be made in writing on a standard form which should be available through county courts. There is currently no charge (though there may be in the future), and neither a solicitor nor a court hearing is required. Once made, the mother cannot change her mind again once the agreement has been lodged with the Principal Registry of the Family Division in London (the address is on the form). Like the order, it can only be ended by the courts.

Both orders and agreements continue even if the relationship between the parents ends, and they give the father exactly the same status as if he were married to the mother. So an 'absent' unmarried father would have to be treated in exactly the same way as a divorced parent *if* he has obtained parental responsibility in either of these ways.

Incomplete information

Schools must therefore have procedures in place for establishing this information for each child. This is not always as difficult as it may sound and it should become easier as the new philosophy takes hold. Primary schools in particular are an essential link in the chain and the better their practice the easier it will be for secondary colleagues. Where a child is in regular contact with the 'absent' parent, this should present little difficulty provided the school asks the right questions from the outset.

Some parents will be reluctant to give the information and there will be little a school can do in response beyond making 'reasonable' efforts. (Exhaustive investigation is not required provided some attempt has been made.) In some circumstances, for example, if the child has not seen the parent concerned for several years, there is little point in reopening old wounds unless the child is keen to re-establish contact.

Even in these circumstances, however, schools could not turn a parent away if they subsequently appear, provided staff are satisfied that they do actually have parental responsibility for the child concerned. In such situations the parent who has the care of the child has a right to know of the approach and should be given an opportunity to take some action themselves, if necessary through the courts. The child's wishes and feelings should be taken into account in deciding what will happen but they may not necessarily be decisive and no child can remove parental responsibility from their parent. Again, only court orders would provide a school with the authority to deny people with parental responsibility that to which they are normally entitled under education law, from parti-cipation in ballots through to parents' consultations. This may also mean a need to be flexible in offering 'absent' parents alternative opportunities for contact with the school or ways of receiving information by post.

In some situations it may prove difficult to collect the information because of the interplay between the Children Act and Child Sup-port Act. Where a mother has been unwilling to give information to the Child Support Agency (and risked loss of benefit as a con-sequence), she is not likely to give such information to a school. 'Absent' parents who are seeking to evade maintenance may also be reluctant to give schools data about themselves, though there is no mention in the Agency's procedures of using school records to trace them. Unmarried fathers are still liable financially even without parental responsibility and it is to be hoped that many 'absent' parents will be keen to be registered at their children's school *as well as* fulfilling these obligations.

The rights of the unmarried father
An unmarried father who has never obtained an order or made an agreement should not, however, be treated as though he has. There is a real difference. He is still a parent and may be offered a range of involvement as such, but, like several other groups of people, he is a parent without parental responsibility. This is true even if the child has his surname and his name is on the birth certificate. In effect the Children Act's definitions mean that he does not have *authority* with respect to the child and so cannot make important decisions. If he has the care of the child he can carry out everyday actions to safe-guard and promote the child's welfare (s3(5)), but this does not

entitle him to act against the wishes of, for example, the child's mother.

If he does not have care of the child his position is extremely vulnerable and schools should probably be guided entirely by the wishes of the mother and any other person who has acquired parental responsibility. If she does not wish him to be involved with the child at all, that is probably her decision to make, and it would be necessary for the father to obtain orders before the school would be under any obligation to consult him. (This is, however, a grey area which needs further legal clarification in relation to entitlements as a parent under education law.)

Step-parents and others

Many other 'parents' who are caring for children will not have parental responsibility for them either, although they may have *written* authority from those with parental responsibility to make decisions on their behalf. (This is a helpful and sensible arrangement which schools may wish to encourage, especially in short-term situations, such as the usual parent–carer being in prison or in hospital or where family relationships have broken down.) But step-parents, for example, do not gain parental responsibility in their own right by marrying a child's actual parent, even if they have lived with them for years and brought them up as their own, and they cannot acquire it by agreement (though this may be possible in future).

So, for example, a child whose mother has divorced and remarried will have three 'parents', only two of whom, his natural mother and father, will have parental responsibility for him. Step-parents and other adults who are bringing up someone else's child, such as grandparents and foster-carers, will only have parental responsibility themselves if they have obtained it via a residence order (see p 72) or by adoption. These cases will be the exception, not the rule. It is extremely important that schools establish the facts of the child's relationships wherever possible; his parents may be called 'Mr and Mrs Smith'; he may call his step-father 'Dad'. This in itself is not enough to tell us exactly who has parental responsibility.

In loco parentis

For day-to-day purposes the above situation may not seem too important as they are all 'parents'. But if what the school requires is the exercise of parental authority it will pay to ensure that appropriate signatures are obtained. Only people with parental responsibility can do this as 'authority' is included in the definition. If you do not have authority you cannot pass it to others. This could be very important if the child has an accident while abroad or the unmarried father tries to move him from one school to another.

School staff do not, of course, have parental responsibility for the children in their care, but the provisions of s2(9) and s3(5) enable those with parental responsibility to arrange for others to carry it out on their behalf and empower any such person to safeguard and promote the child's welfare. So, provided such delegation has taken place, school staff should feel in a strong position to exercise a degree of authority and control over such children where required. This role still carries considerable significance. It would, for example, enable a member of staff to consent to surgery during a school visit or refuse to hand over the child to a parent who was drunk or violent, pending a more permanent solution of the problem.

But this makes it even more important that schools have obtained the correct authorization to act, in order to be sure that the persons asking them to exercise their parental responsibility for them actually have it themselves. It is certainly good practice for forms dealing with admissions, trips involving anything hazardous or any overnight stays, or any other important issues, to carry a notice such as *'This form should be signed by someone with parental responsibility'*, together with a brief outline of what this means. (This is becoming more commonplace with respect to medical decisions/consent to surgery for children.)

Incorrect action would then be the responsibility of the person signing the form rather than the school. Not specifying the requirement could, however, leave the school vulnerable, if people without parental responsibility give permission which others, who actually have it but were not asked, might not have done. (The education group CALIG, the Children Act Implementation Group in London, is doing more work at present on which educational decisions *require* the action of someone with parental responsibility and which can be made by any parent. This is an area about which it is difficult to be precise.)

This is where step-parents who have never obtained a residence order or adopted the child may feel at least partially excluded from the child's life, though they are still 'parents' and should be treated as such. There are those, including STEPFAMILY, the national support organization for step-parents, who have suggested that the Act has got things wrong here and there is some pressure for amendment to allow step-parents to share parental responsibility by agreement as an unmarried father can do. However, this is not available at present. Not being the child's natural parent does make a significant legal difference and neither schools nor parents would be acting appropriately if they ignored this fact.

Where there is no one with parental responsibility

This is not so unusual, eg, an unmarried father bringing up his child after the mother's death where there is no agreement or order in force, or grandparents caring for the child of their unmarried daughter whose whereabouts are unknown and where the arrangements have never been legally recognized. Schools which are exercising quality pastoral care in such circumstances, especially where they are long-term arrangements, will want to discuss with carers who are not actual parents whether they wish to acquire parental responsibility for the child in order to increase their sense of stability.

Short of adoption this can only be done through the making of a residence order, normally in the context of a dispute, but Government guidance suggests that orders might also be made to promote the child's welfare in this way. Without such action there is a significant vacuum with respect to the child where no one is available who actually has the legal right to make decisions on their behalf. Not all commentators and practitioners see this as a problem, though it leaves schools in particular in a very difficult position. As elsewhere, solicitors experienced in family law should be able to advise.

Parents and guardians

If everyone with parental responsibility for the child has died, the child may have a guardian who has taken it over from them. Anyone can appoint a guardian for a child for whom they are legally responsible, but such appointments only take effect when *all* those with parental responsibility are dead. So, a guardian does not take over if the divorced parent with whom the child is living dies if there is another parent with parental responsibility still alive. The exception is where a sole residence order has been made (see p 72) in favour of the person who has died, in which case they could still nominate a guardian to take over in the event of their death, but *as well as* any other living parent, not instead of them. *Because of the rarity of these situations, 'Parent or Guardian' is no longer a helpful phrase on forms etc.* Either 'parent' (for general use) or 'person with parental responsibility' (for major decisions) is now much to be preferred.

Children 'in care'

Children who are being 'looked after' by the local authority will also raise questions about parental responsibility. It is extremely important that school staff appreciate the difference between children who are 'accommodated' under s20 and children who are 'in care' by virtue of a care order under s31. Only children on a care order made by a court are 'in care'. Where a child is accommodated, *all* the parental responsibility remains with the parents; neither the foster-carers nor the local authority acquire it.

If the child is on a care order, the local authority will have parental responsibility *as well as* the parents, not instead of them as would have happened in care proceedings prior to the Children Act. In practice, the SSD will determine the extent of the parents' involvement and it could be radically curtailed, but they should not necessarily be ignored altogether unless the circumstances demand it. They retain rights with respect to their child's education unless the child's welfare requires that they be set aside. (For example, their consent should still be sought if their child needs assessment by an educational psychologist.)

SECTION 8 ORDERS

Custody and access abolished

Section 8 orders are an important part of the legislation and may have significant effects on a child's education. They may be made in both private and public law proceedings. In part they are the replacement for custody and access, but two new orders add to the scope of their use. The courts may make these orders in the course of established proceedings, such as divorce, either on their own initiative or by application, or they may be made on 'free standing' applications with no other proceedings involved. Parents can apply for any of these orders and other people, including children, who can satisfy the court that they have a genuine interest in the child's welfare and that they understand what they are doing, can apply for a residence or contact order. Local authorities may seek leave to apply for a prohibited steps order or a specific issue order. This will be rare but may provide a way of resolving a dispute about a child with the minimum level of court intervention.

Courts will not make an order at all unless they are satisfied that it will be of positive benefit to the child. Most couples will separate or divorce without the need for any orders, provided they can agree on the arrangements for their children, so in most 'split family' situations *there will be no restrictions at all* on each parent remaining involved. Where there are orders, it is quite reasonable for schools to ask to see and to keep copies in circumstances where their existence may be relevant in defining pastoral practice. It is best not to rely on word of mouth as misunderstandings could easily occur.

Residence orders: settling where a child lives

A residence order may be made either because there has been a dispute (between the parents or between the parents and someone else, including the child), or because there has been a question about the child's welfare which has needed an order to settle the arrangements. They have several major implications for schools detailed below.

Changes in parental responsibility
Anyone who is named on a residence order as living with the child and caring for them, obtains parental responsibility for them with the making of the order (s12). Unlike people who have parental responsibility as of right, they lose it again once the order ends. In general, therefore, they will lose it once the child is 16. This could be a very significant issue for a school if there is no one then left with parental responsibility for the child while they still have several months of compulsory education remaining or if previous disputes are reopened at this crucial time in a child's life. There is provision for an extension of this limit, though at present it has not been established whether this situation would constitute the 'exceptional' circumstances which the Act says must be present for a section 8 order to extend past 16.

The making of a residence order does not remove anyone's parental responsibility; it simply adds in new people for as long as the order lasts. So it will be perfectly possible for a child to have three or four people who *all* have parental responsibility for him, each of whom has the right to exercise it independently, each of whom should be treated as a parent: for example, two formerly married partners, neither of whom live with their child *and* his two grandparents who are actually bringing him up and have obtained a residence order. (Even without an order, such a child would still have four adults entitled to be recorded by the school as 'registered parents' and treated as such, though the legal authority would lie only with the actual parents, wherever they are.)

Where a step-parent has acquired parental responsibility in this way, school staff must be careful to remember that the child's actual parent who no longer lives with him may have it as well. During the course of a child's school career there may be several changes in who has parental responsibility for him as his circumstances change. School records will need to be carefully managed to make sure that information is both accurate and up to date and that people are treated appropriately.

Many applications for residence orders will, in effect, be applications for parental responsibility by people who have no other means of obtaining it, other than the much more final (and expensive) alternative of adoption. This concept should also see the end of 'mother's own' adoptions in which the natural mother who remarried had to adopt her own child in order to enable her new husband to acquire legal responsibility for him. Residence orders should mean fewer adoptions generally where people are willing to share parental responsibility rather than wishing to take it over entirely. All those with parental responsibility must be consulted about these applications, though consent is not necessarily required if the court feels the order is in the child's best interests.

Applications by children
Issues to do with residence and parental responsibility have usually been the question at stake in the well-publicized cases where children have initiated the proceedings themselves, which they have every right to do if the court is satisfied that they understand what they are doing. There is no lower age limit, though 12 seems to be emerging by consensus so far. In these cases there is a dispute about who should be exercising authority with respect to the child and they have asked the court to resolve the matter by determining what arrangements are in their best interests.

Although these cases have created quite a stir, there is really nothing exceptional about them and this process will probably become more commonplace in time. Helping a child through the process may well be a role for pastoral staff and others who wish to encourage him to settle issues which are affecting his welfare. Older children in particular may wish to make changes in arrangements for their care and, if their application is disputed, they may ask staff to support them or to comment on their experience of the other parties involved. The question of their 'educational needs' may also be relevant.

Changes of surname
If a child is subject to a residence order, he may not be known by a new surname without either leave of the court or the consent of *all* those with parental responsibility (s13). This is also true of old custody orders (though nobody took much notice), but it is much

more important in the changed climate of the Children Act with its emphasis on equal parental participation. Schools are frequently asked to 'change children's names' when new relationships begin or old ones end. In general it is wise to be cautious.

If there is a residence order, no changes can be made without written consent. Those who *must* consent include, for example, the actual father of a child in a new step-family where his former wife wishes the child to be known by the surname of her new husband. This seems entirely reasonable and schools should not make changes without such consent. It is not appropriate that someone discovers later that a child for whom they have parental responsibility is now being called by a new surname at school without their knowledge. That does not adequately reflect the new balance of responsibility and parents in such a position would rightly feel that the school had not been even-handed. Even without a residence order good practice would suggest that consultation should take place before making any changes.

Even then we are only talking about a change to the 'name by which the child is known', not a change to their legal name. The original name should still be retained in admission registers etc as in 'John Smith (known as Brown)'. 'John Brown' would not adequately reflect the position, though that form might be used informally. On the whole schools should advise parents that they cannot 'change children's names'. If parents or children wish to make a permanent change to be used in all circumstances, they should be advised to see a solicitor about making a 'statutory declaration' or a change by certificate of deed poll. This is far preferable to making a cosmetic change which may suggest that certain parent(s) no longer feature in a child's life without the parent(s) being given an opportunity to object. In most situations this will be a question of good practice; where there is a residence order, schools would be breaking the law by making changes without proper prior consultation.

Contact orders: the child's right to contact

These define the arrangements by which a child will have contact with someone who is named on the order and with whom they do not live. This will usually be a parent but could equally be a grandparent or sibling. The emphasis is intended to be different from the old access orders in that the contact arrangements are to be seen from the child's perspective rather than the parent's. They define his right to contact with them rather than the other way round, though it is difficult to see how they could force someone to have contact who did not wish to do so. As with all section 8 orders they will not be made unless they are necessary but, usually in the context of a dispute, they will define the nature and frequency of the contact, which may include overnight stays. Contact may be defined by means of telephone calls or letters as well as face-to-face meetings.

These will not normally be of great significance for schools, except perhaps those with boarding facilities where contact arrangements may affect the child at weekends. There may be circumstances in which the school is asked to facilitate the contact and so staff would need to have details of the order, again in writing. A child might, for example, be met by a parent on a Friday afternoon as set out in the order and then returned to school on the Sunday or Monday. Restrictions on contact are more likely to be defined by a prohibited steps order (see below). If there are no orders, contact can be at any reasonable time to be negotiated. *No order does not mean no contact.*

Prohibited steps orders: restricting parental responsibility

These prevent the taking of some action which would otherwise be a quite reasonable exercise of parental responsibility. If, for example, the parent who has the care of the child is concerned that the other parent may seek to abduct him or cause him physical violence, they may have obtained one of these orders to prohibit the 'absent' parent from having any contact with the child except by prior arrangement and under supervision. Clearly in these situations in particular it is essential that parents inform the child's school of the order and that a copy is kept on their personal file.

With such an order in force, a school could refuse the parent's request to come and see the child at school. Without such an order, while the school could delay their intervention or suggest that it was not appropriate to disrupt the child's day, staff would have no grounds for turning the parent away altogether, providing their actions were reasonable. (It is always possible for parents to be asked to leave school premises if they are being unreasonable or violent or to be required to make a convenient appointment.)

It is important to be clear that only what is prohibited may be denied. Even these orders do not take parental responsibility away. It very much depends what the order actually says, which is why schools will need a copy. It may not be the case that *all* involvement with the child is prohibited, only certain things. Even a parent who is prohibited from having any direct contact with the child might still be entitled, for example, to information by post about their progress. Sometimes information is provided with the name of the school erased or reports etc are sent via a solicitor or to prisons. All of this will present no problem to any school which is confident that it knows where the boundaries are. If the order exists without the school's knowledge, or if its restrictions are ignored, this could create serious difficulties, not only for the school but also, potentially, for the child.

Admission forms

A prohibited steps order might prohibit a parent from changing the child's school or taking them away on holiday. The normal rules of parental responsibility may not apply if, for example, there is an order which says that the parent is not to know where the child is living or they are not to contact their school. Although this may be considered difficult to put into practice, schools should not feel diffident about asking parents to tell them the child's full circumstances on admission and to keep them informed of any changes. There should be a specific question on admission forms about whether there are any court orders which relate to the child. If a parent chooses not to pass on information when asked to do so, then *they* might reasonably be held responsible for any mistakes made subsequently. If the school has never asked the question it could be a different matter.

Specific issue orders: deciding a dispute

These resolve particular areas of disagreement about the exercise of parental responsibility towards the child. Experience has already shown that many of these involve education. Parents are faced with a wide range of choices and inevitably these may become the focus of disagreement between them. There is a greatly increased risk that such issues may have to be resolved by orders rather than by negotiation if changes are made to a child's educational provision without all those who have a right to be consulted having an opportunity to influence what is decided.

If a parent is excluded from the decision-making process, and then discovers later that something has happened with which they do not agree, they may seek to overturn that decision by means of a specific issue order. Choice of school is the most obvious example and procedures should exist to ensure that *all* those with parental responsibility for a child have a chance to express their wishes, even if ultimately one parent has to make the decision. People who feel that they have at least been heard are less likely to rush to the courts for satisfaction.

These last two orders can be made *ex parte*; that is, in the absence of one or other of the parties who would normally have a right to be there. There have certainly been examples of a parent convincing the court that the matter at stake was so urgent that an interim order must be made immediately, even without the knowledge of the other parent. (One example was of a child who was delivered to school in the morning by one parent; by the afternoon the other parent had produced an order entitling them to meet the child from school!)

These orders do not, in my judgement at least, always appear to have been based on the best interests of the child as the Act requires, but, once made, they must be complied with until they are amended or removed. Schools may find that a parent produces an interim order out of the blue enabling them to enforce one side of a dispute or to take some action which the school does not necessarily believe to be in line with the child's welfare. There is little choice but to comply. Hopefully a more considered review will then take place in which the school, in line with the 'welfare checklist', should be given an opportunity to have its say.

THE STAFFORDSHIRE RESPONSE

Managing pupil data

As all schools are required by law to collect and store data about pupils' 'parents', these complex issues raise major questions about the quality of every school's pupil data system and how it is administered. The model presented in figure 3.2 for helping schools and parents to share the necessary information is not intended to be definitive. Different circumstances may require different ways of responding, but this approach is offered as one way in which an LEA and local schools have co-operated in ensuring a reasonable standard of good practice where the Children Act is concerned. Basically three areas of information are required:

- Who has parental responsibility for the child and, if they do not live with the child, where do they live?
- Who lives with the child and which of them has parental responsibility for him (they are all 'parents')?
- Are there any court orders which relate to the child (excluding adoption orders which need not be disclosed separately)?

Two points need to be stressed at the outset. First, this is not simply a process of collecting data. If parents are to be asked to give schools

raising awareness/ stimulating demand	– senior LEA Officers – information in LEA publications/ brochures for parents

training	– headteachers, pastoral staff/governors
	  through literature circulated to schools/
	  central events through Inspectorate/
	  individual school and pyramid
	  presentations

consultation	– Consultative Committees – other agencies/courts etc
preparation of resources	– (minority languages? Media coverage?) – provided for each school:

(a) data collection form for each child to
   take home covering who lives with
   the child, who has parental
   responsibility, anyone else with
   parental responsibility living at a
   different address, and whether there
   are any orders which relate to the
   child

(b) an information leaflet about the Act
   and parental responsibility for each
   child to take home

(c) a draft letter for schools to send out
   on their own notepaper explaining the
   purpose of the exercise

(d) follow-up letters to be sent to 'absent'
   parents when data is collected about
   them

distribution to schools	– by EWOs/centrally printed/collated
support to schools/ parents during the collection period	– 'Helpline' to deal with enquiries – follow-up visits by EWOs as required – clinics to deal with enquiries at school level

on-going
support longer
term
	– contact points for further enquiries by
	  parents and schools
	– advice re information in school brochures
	– further training esp for school governors
	  on drawing up whole school policies
	– updating of records (SIMS Star 3
	  package)

Figure 3.2 *Data collection process in Staffordshire schools*

personal details about their family circumstances and the status of their children, it must be appreciated that for many this will be a painful process. There may be secrets hidden in the life of the family which have never been disclosed – 'How can I tell the school that the man I live with is not my son's father when I haven't told my son!' There will be feelings of anger – 'What do you mean I don't have parental responsibility for this girl; I've brought her up for years without so much as a penny from her real father!' There will be refusal to co-operate – 'I've kept their mother away from them for the last two years and I'm not letting her back in now!' And there will be simple misunderstandings – 'Of course I've got parental responsibility; I'm his father!' Both parents and schools will require support and professional expertise in order to make the exercise worthwhile.

Second, this should be seen as a complete process in which no part may be left out. It needs to begin at the beginning and continue till the end. Starting in the middle, without adequate preparation and training, or finishing before the end without on-going support would be courting disaster. The whole sequence would take several months to carry through (see also Appendix 1).

Putting it into practice

Staffordshire, a county containing both rural and urban/inner city areas, began from the perspective of almost 150,000 children in over 500 schools, spread over a wide geographical area. Following initial training, there had been consistent demand from headteachers across the county for a centrally managed process to assist them in collecting the data. This immediately sets the context for a project on rather a grand scale which might not be appropriate elsewhere. The education welfare service, based in several local centres, consists of approximately 60 officers, including eight area officers and two specialist officers, specifically appointed to assist both the LEA and its schools to implement new ways of working in response to the Children Act. Not all LEAs would have such resources available.

Some mistakes were made, as with all innovative work, particularly in the amount of time allowed for prior consultation outside the education service. Not every agency was ready for the flood of enquiries which the exercise created. Some of the local media coverage was sensationalist and unhelpful, though some, especially on local radio, was immensely valuable in communicating the aims of the exercise. Not all headteachers and schools proved to be committed to the task and, of course, some parents did not respond. But on the whole, schools seemed happy with the programme which was offered and grateful that they had not simply been left to manage the issues on their own.

The major cost was the production of 150,000 forms and explanatory leaflets, enough for every child to take home one of each (see figure 3.3). This cost was not passed on to schools, though schools were invited to photocopy standard letters onto their own notepaper and many incurred additional postage, especially when sending information to 'absent' parents of whom they were previously unaware.

'Helpline'

The telephone 'helpline' was staffed by education welfare officers who had received special training and operated up to 7pm Monday–Thursday. During the five-week period when the vast majority of schools sent out the information, 1,249 enquiries were dealt with. This enabled many questions to be deflected from the schools where the time and expertise to answer them might not have been available. It also made sure that parents, many of whom were initially hostile to the exercise when they rang, received efficient and well-informed help. Many other enquiries were dealt with by the officers in the course of their normal duties.

In most cases it proved possible to reassure those who had anxieties about the process or to reach some reasonable compromise in the light of their particular situation. The callers tended to be those whose circumstances were the most complicated and the whole process clearly demonstrated just how complex some children's lives are. Most callers seemed to understand the information which they had been given, even if they did not like what they had been told! Some actually expressed appreciation that either they or their former partner were now being given an opportunity to participate in their child's education. Many callers were advised to speak to a solicitor about whether private law orders were needed or given information about how to make a parental responsibility agreement – information which surely ought to be much more widely available through local Registrars etc than appears to be the case.

Confidentiality

Parents may well be giving schools details about which, quite reasonably, they want some assurance of confidentiality. There were obvious examples such as: 'I've told my daughter that her father is abroad, when in fact, he's in prison,' or 'Everyone thinks we're

<u>**Staffordshire**</u>
County Council

Child's Name _____ **d.o.b.** _____

Address _____
_____ **Postcode** _____ **Tel:** _____

School _____

PLEASE READ THE ENCLOSED LEAFLET CAREFULLY BEFORE COMPLETING THIS FORM

1. The following adults live with the child and act as parent:

Full Name	Relationship to child	Do they have parental responsibility ?
		YES/NO
		YES/NO
		YES/NO
		YES/NO
		YES/NO

2. The following adults have " parental responsibility " but do not live with the child:

Full Name	Relationship to child	Address

3. Are there any Court Orders which relate to the child? e.g. custody orders/Section 8 Orders under the Children Act 1989 **YES/NO**

If **YES** please say what they are:

_____
_____

This information will be transferred into the school's computer system. Under the Data Protection Act 1984, anyone named above has the right to know that information about them has been collected and given an opportunity to check its accuracy.

This form should be signed by someone with parental responsibility wherever possible.

Please return it to the school as soon as possible.

Signed _____ **Relationship to child** _____

Date _____

Figure 3.3 *Data collection form*

married and we don't want them to know we're not.' This is clearly a very important issue for pastoral practice within the school and there should be clear procedures which establish who needs to know the information and for what purpose. There may even be questions about how data is passed backwards and forwards between the school and the home if, for example, staff are party to something which the child does not know about. It is vital that schools seek to establish a trusting relationship with parents in order to be able to give appropriate reassurances while still being free to act on the information which has been given.

Data protection

Many schools store pupil data by means of a computer. (One of the reasons why few schools have yet come to terms with the issues raised by the Act is because new programs designed to take account of the changes have been so long in coming. These will require answers to Children Act questions and therefore some kind of publicity exercise for parents will be needed to enable them to know how to reply.) If one parent gives the school information about another parent, which is held on the school's computer, the latter has the right to know that data has been collected about them.

It is therefore good practice to ensure that they are aware of the fact, either through their former partner, or, if necessary, by post. This is a very useful opportunity as it also provides a chance to offer a range of options to 'absent' parents and to reach agreement with them about how they wish to be involved in their child's education in future. This then forestalls any risk that they may subsequently claim to have been ignored. Insufficient data makes this approach impossible and risks future crises, though clearly there are resource implications here, especially for larger schools.

Empowerment

Part of the difficulty facing schools is that, at present, staff occupy the front line in telling people that the law has changed. It was clear from this exercise that many people were not aware of the existence of the Act, nor of its significance for their personal circumstances. The whole exercise may be seen as one of empowerment; enabling parents and children to decide what action to take once they are in full possession of the facts. If parents are so important in education, why has there been no attempt to make sure that they are aware of their rights? Have the implications of all this parental power over schools ever been discussed between the DoH and the DfE?

It is unfortunate that there has been so little public debate or information about the Children Act's provisions. In time this should become less of a problem as parents will already have been asked about parental responsibility through, for example, health services or when first registering their child at a school. But in the short term this process certainly revealed that there are large numbers of people who need help and advice and that schools are inevitably the place where they look to find it because that is where the questions have to be asked. While all of this could easily be seen as a nuisance – one more burden for hard-pressed teaching and administrative staff – it is surely best seen as an opportunity, even when it means four 'parents' to cope with at a consultation evening! Good practice here may, in the end, lead to better-adjusted children and more responsive parents. That must be in everyone's interests.

CASE STUDIES

Many of the changes in pastoral practice required by the Children Act are best illustrated by case studies. While they are always in danger of creating caricatures – trying to condense complex issues into just a few words – such studies do put some flesh on these rather dry bones and make the implications of all this clearer. The following examples are all based on real situations with the names changed. They illustrate the range of situations where problems may arise unless teachers and others pay attention to the Act's provisions. While waiting for the crisis to come is one way of handling pastoral care and the involvement of parents, common sense suggests that it will be better for everyone involved, including school staff but especially for the child, if these potential flashpoints are anticipated. Otherwise a great deal of time and effort may be expended in undoing what should not have been done in the first place.

Each of the studies has a heading which illustrates the main point being made. They tend rather to overemphasize the significance of court orders, but those are the examples which cause teachers most anxiety and where practice needs to be at its best!

Independent action

Marie's father contacts the headteacher and demands an appointment. He works away from home a lot and, during a recent absence, his wife gave permission for Marie to visit a mosque as part of her religious studies course. He makes it clear to the headteacher that he does not approve of the visit and would not have given permission if he had been at home. He demands that the head overturns his wife's approval and says he forbids her to go. The head confirms that the father does have parental responsibility for Marie, but would have to advise him that both he and his wife have equal authority and that she can make the decision without his consent. An attempt to resolve the question by negotiation would be attempted. If that failed, the head would have to back one parent or the other. He/she could consult Marie to see what she wanted to do or choose whichever alternative was felt to be in her best interests.

Restricting parental responsibility

Sarah and Mark have just been admitted to a small rural school by their mother. On admission, the school establishes that they have different fathers. Mark's father is unknown (unmarried) but Sarah's mother is still married to her father. The family has been moving around the country to escape what the mother says is serious violence from her husband. She does not want him to know where the children are and refuses to give the school any details about him, even though he has parental responsibility for Sarah (only). There are no orders in force. The head is able to reassure the mother that her husband has no rights with respect to Mark at all, but also explains that if Sarah's father were to contact the school himself, he could not at present be denied reasonable involvement with Sarah's education. This need not necessarily include giving him the children's address and the head agrees not to do so without the mother's permission. It might be better if the mother seeks an injunction or a prohibited steps order to set clear limits on her husband's actions. This could be done *ex parte* if she can convince the court of the urgency of the situation, but it would take the pressure off the school and keep the responsibility with the mother acting through the court.

Limits on unmarried fathers

Sebastian goes to stay with his father for half-term. His father was never married to his mother and she has a custody order from before the Children Act. At the end of the holiday, the father refuses to return Sebastian home, despite a phone call from the mother demanding that he do so. The father claims that Sebastian is unhappy living with his mother and wants to live with him now. After a few days. Sebastian is taken to the school near where his father lives for admission. The school should establish that his father does not have parental responsibility for him and so does not have the authority to change Sebastian's school without his mother's permission. It would be best if the parents could agree new arrangements together, but if this is not possible, orders will be needed to settle where Sebastian should live and whether his father should obtain parental responsibility for him. If the father refused to return him home, his mother could seek orders prohibiting her former partner from having Sebastian with him or changing his school. Sebastian's own wishes and feelings should be considered in the light of his age and understanding.

The 'mature minor'/residence orders

Julie is 14 and, after an argument with her parents, has moved out of the family home to live with her boyfriend and his parents. He is 17 and has just left the same school where Julie is registered. She is now refusing to go to school and her parents are generally concerned for her welfare. The Social Services Department has offered to help with counselling etc, but, having visited Julie, the social worker does not feel that she is at any risk of 'significant harm' so there is no question of care proceedings. Her parents decide to apply for a residence order so that the court can determine where Julie should live. Julie and her boyfriend's parents are considering asking for leave to make a counter-application for an order saying she can stay where she is. The court will take her wishes and feelings very seriously, but will have to determine the issue according to what is in her best interests. The issue of her education should be considered as part of the duty to apply the welfare checklist and the LEA may be asked to report on whether it considers an education supervision order to be appropriate. Alternatively, the LEA could consider initiating an application itself in order to get the case into family proceedings. School staff may also be asked to assist the court with information about both sets of parents from their experience of them.

Specific issue orders

Shanjit's parents are separated but still married and she lives with her father. He is still taking her each day to the school which she used to attend when the family all lived together, some 12 miles away. After informing his wife of his intentions, Shanjit's father decides to move her to the school near where she now lives so that she can be with all her new friends. He admits her on the first day of the new term, explaining that he is separated and giving his wife's name and address. Later in the morning, with the second post, the school receives a copy of a specific issue order made the previous day *ex parte* on the application of his wife, without her husband's knowledge. This rules that Shanjit must stay at the school where she was previously registered, pending a final hearing to determine the question. Her father and the school must do what the order says, so she has to be removed from the roll, at least temporarily, and returned to her original school.

Changing children's surnames

Leroy's father has contacted the education offices to complain that the school which Leroy attends has changed his surname without his permission. Leroy's parents are divorced and his mother has recently remarried. She and her second husband have arranged with the school that they would 'change his name so that he would be the same as their own child'. His ex-wife has 'custody', but Leroy's mother is considering obtaining one of the new residence orders so that her new husband can be his 'proper' dad. The school has made a mistake in allowing the change of name. The most they should have done is to change his 'known by' name and Leroy's father should have been asked for his consent first. They must continue to use Leroy's real surname for official purposes unless he has it legally changed. The EWO who took the phone call would advise his father that a condition of the residence order would be that no change could be made without his permission. Even without the order it would not be good practice to ignore his objections and things should really be left as they were originally unless he and his ex-wife can come to some new arrangement. If Leroy feels strongly enough about it, he can initiate a legal change but it's not likely to happen without his real father's consent.

The welfare checklist

Jenny is in family proceedings because her parents are divorcing and they cannot agree about where she should live and the contact arrangements. She is currently living with her mother in the previous family home and attends a special day school for children with physical and sensory disabilities. The court welfare officer has written to the Educational Psychology Service, and to her current school, asking for detailed reports about her educational needs and the kind of setting in which they should be met. She is also asking about what effect a change might have on Jenny at this time and whether there are suitable educational facilities available near to where her father intends to live.

Treating parents equally

Colin is having contact with his father at the weekend. His parents divorced a year ago. On the Saturday afternoon they go out for a drive, and, in the course of the journey, Colin points out what he says is his new school. It is a Roman Catholic day school. His father, who is not a Roman Catholic, establishes that his mother moved him to the school six weeks ago but had forgotten to tell him. She says she gave the school his name and address on admission but it seems they have made no attempt to contact him. Colin's father is unhappy about this, and about the fact that he was not consulted prior to the move being made. His ex-wife is quite willing to encourage his involvement and this should present no problem provided everyone shares the necessary information and then acts upon it. Colin's father would have to feel very strongly before a court would consider making any orders overturning his ex-wife's decision, but he might be less likely to choose this option if he had been consulted and involved by the school all along.

Incorrect pupil data

William has received two short-term exclusions from school recently and his year head is worried that he may be excluded permanently unless his behaviour improves. After consulting the EWO, they decide to call a meeting with William's parents to discuss his problems and to try and prevent things getting worse. On William's records it says that he lives with Mr and Mrs Anderson and William is registered with the same surname. When the EWO visits to confirm the arrangements for the meeting, she also explains about parental responsibility and asks who has it with respect to William. For the first time his mother says that his surname isn't really Anderson and that her present husband is not his father but his step-father. William still sees his father every few weeks but she considered it unnecessary to tell the school about him, having been divorced for six years. It will be good practice to try and get all three 'parents' involved in putting a plan together to address William's behavioural problems. His relationship with his father could be part of the reason behind the problem and not involving him may be leaving out the person who actually has the power to change things. The school could also use this opportunity to establish with William's father how he wishes to be involved in his son's education in future.

Parents' rights

Pauline's father contacts the chair of governors at her school to complain that he hasn't been receiving any reports about her progress and wasn't informed about a recent governors' election. He claims to have contacted the headteacher on two occasions asking for opportunities to be involved in her education but that nothing has happened in response. On checking Pauline's records, there is no information about her father at all, just 'divorced' written on her card. It seems that Pauline's mother has always refused to give any information about him and gave the school instructions that, if he ever contacted them, they were to do nothing about it. This way of dealing with the issue will have to change, either by encouraging Pauline's mother to recognize that her ex-husband still has some rights, to be sorted out by negotiation, or, if necessary, by the school making independent arrangements with him. Only a court order could enable the school to prohibit him from reasonable involvement. Pauline's wishes should be heard but need not necessarily be decisive.

4

Absence from School

THE LEGAL CONTEXT

The problem with 'truancy'

Children are not breaking the law if they fail to attend school regularly. There is no offence of 'truancy' and a child cannot be brought before any criminal court on the grounds that he has skipped school. This may come as rather bad news to hard-pressed teachers trying to motivate children who are frequently absent. Only parents can commit an offence. They have a legal duty to ensure that children under the minimum school-leaving age attend regularly at the school where they are registered, and they can be prosecuted and fined for failing to do so. Clearly such an approach is only appropriate when it is the parent, not the child, who has failed to act responsibly. Otherwise we are likely to end up rewarding the child for his behaviour by doing exactly what he wants us to do – punishing the parent!

This lack of legal sanction against children is not usually recognized in national debate about how to deal with juvenile offending. 'Truancy' is often included as part of the criminal behaviour which may require a punitive response. The fact that such an approach is not available because truancy is not an offence, causes some difficulty, especially, for example, if the child is already being looked after by the local authority or if the parents have done everything reasonably possible to encourage his attendance.

There are some arguments for making older children responsible for their behaviour in exactly the same way as they are expected to obey other laws, against shoplifting for example. But there would be difficulties of another kind if not going to school were made a criminal offence by the child. To begin with, there would be endless wrangles about definitions. It is impossible to isolate 'truancy' from all the other reasons why children miss school. What is the difference between 'truancy' and 'school refusal'? What about children who leave school *after* registration? Schools apply widely differing definitions in categorizing absences and absence often has a variety of interacting explanations. Which would be an offence? What punishments could be applied anyway?

A welfare approach

The 'welfare' approach is much to be preferred; seeing poor attendance as damaging the best interests of the child and trying to understand what is actually going on in the child's behaviour so that he can be helped to change it. Only then can we know whether there is an answer and which course of action is most appropriate. Not all 'truants' have a problem; some of them, quite rightly, sense that what is on offer does not meet their needs. Not all children with attendance problems are 'truants' and they should not be regarded as such.

Thanks to the Children Act, the title 'education welfare officer' no longer carries nineteenth-century paternalistic overtones. It actually describes their job – promoting the welfare of children at school, the 'paramount' consideration when deciding how to deal with children's problems. Many, however, prefer 'education social worker' and the terms are often used interchangeably as the work of an EWO/ESW undoubtedly involves the exercise of social-work skills. Either term represents an advance over 'School Board Man' which is still used by some parents and schools! Only officers of the LEA can act in the courts. Some schools are experimenting with employing their own 'truant officers', but they, of course, have no statutory powers at all and their legal position is highly uncertain should parents choose not to co-operate with them.

Tackling absence from school has to be understood against three different legal contexts, not all of which are based on the welfare principle, but each of which is involved in setting the boundaries for action. Education welfare officers/social workers have to operate in the nexus of these three approaches. It is essential that teachers are familiar with them if there is to be effective working together.

Education Act 1993

The duties of parents
This Act simply restates the provisions of the 1944 Education Act

about offences by parents. Attending a school is not compulsory. LEAs, for example, now have a duty to make alternative provision if needed. Parents are free to educate their children 'otherwise' than at school and many choose to do so. However, they must then satisfy the LEA that the education is appropriate for their child's needs and fulfils legal requirements. If no such agreement is reached, and the child remains unregistered at any school, the LEA can serve a school attendance order, usually giving the parents a choice of schools. Failure to respond to such an order is an offence. These are very rare.

Once children become registered pupils at a school, parents have a duty to ensure their regular attendance. The Children Act abolished imprisonment as a sanction for not doing so and parents are normally conditionally discharged or fined if convicted of the offence in a magistrates' court. The maximum fine for an offence at level 3 is £1,000 but, in practice, fines are far smaller, sometimes as little as £10–20, especially if the parents are on a low income or dependent on benefits. There are various statutory defences such as the school having granted leave, sickness, days for religious observance and the LEA not having fulfilled its duty to provide transport where required to do so.

Limits to prosecution
While prosecution of parents appears popular with the Government (and with some headteachers), there is little proof that either the use or the threat of it is very effective, except in circumstances where the root problem is parental failure to act responsibly and parents are able to pay a significant fine. In my experience at least, such an easy answer is rarely appropriate. Far from acting as a deterrent, prosecutions which result in discharges or derisory fines may actually prove counter-productive in reinforcing the importance of education. If prosecution does not change the situation, what happens next? The action can easily be made to look ridiculous. Fines on poor people who are already deep in debt only increase the stress within the family and result in the child being faced with additional problems.

As well as all this, some schools may now be reluctant to provide the LEA with the evidence it needs and, in a sense, the onus has now shifted on to them to prove that the absences were illegitimate. In the past, the mere fact of absence was sufficient unless the parent could prove otherwise. Now, only certain kinds of absences may be used as evidence (see p 99). This shift of emphasis is an interesting, albeit unintended, complement to the Children Act's principle of non-intervention, though the DfE still seems to expect LEAs to act as if the opposite were true.

'Truancy sweeps'

It is because the focus of any offence is on the parent rather than the child, that EWOs/ESWs have generally been less than enthusiastic about trying to deal with non-attendance at school by patrols in shopping centres etc. There is no obvious legal power which gives the Police or anyone else the right to stop a child on the street and detain him on suspicion of being absent from school without authority. Even if there were, how would such children be distinguished from those who are on home tuition, on their way back from a hospital appointment, on holiday for a staff training day or sent home from school because the boiler has broken down? In reality, certain kinds of children would be targeted because they 'looked' like truants according to a variety of preconceived ideas and stereotypes and much confusion, timewasting and ill feeling could result.

Those schemes which have some merit focus on the *welfare* issues and Police involvement is strictly limited. Children who refuse to go with officers when challenged are not removed physically against their will. Referral is made immediately, with the co-operation of the child, to professional social work staff, who ensure that appropriate responses are made. Some parents who are failing in their duty to ensure their child is educated might be identified in this way; some children who are genuinely at risk of 'significant harm' while loitering in town centres might be more effectively protected.

In practice, however, many of the children approached will already be excluded or 'looked after' by the local authority and so little might be achieved. The chances are that any 'truants' who are determined not to be discovered will easily be able to avoid detection or will simply spend their time elsewhere, perhaps in even more dangerous places. In my judgement, few long-term answers to the questions children are asking us by staying away from school will be found through this route.

The Children Act 1989

Court direction

Instead of, or as well as, dealing with the issue as an offence by the parents, a magistrates' court can direct the LEA to apply for an education supervision order (ESO) with respect to the child. ESOs can only be made on application and the LEA has no power to apply directly for any other orders. Children cannot become the subject of care proceedings by direction in this way as magistrates' courts used to be able to do with the old juvenile courts before the Children Act. If a court makes such a direction to seek an ESO, the LEA must respond within eight weeks and indicate what other action is being taken to promote the child's welfare if an order is not being applied for. The order lasts for a year but can be extended by up to three more (see p 100 for detailed provision).

New ways of working
Despite first impressions, however, this is not the most important implication of the Act in terms of tackling problems with school attendance, because, in line with its general aim of ensuring that all possible voluntary means have been exhausted first, the whole context in which agencies may intervene in children's lives has been substantially changed. Action in the courts of any kind will be rare and new powers in that area are a side-issue for the vast majority of children with attendance difficulties. The important thing is ensuring that we are promoting their welfare, in partnership with the child and his parents wherever possible, in exactly the same way as other agencies would do. Courts are not the answer except in a very small minority of cases. There is a whole range of other interventions available which should be explored before any statutory action by the LEA or anyone else should be undertaken (see figure 4.1).

Most problems can be resolved by the provision of services and the negotiation of agreements. Just as the SSD would not consider using statutory powers unless they are absolutely necessary, LEAs and schools should ensure that they have given other approaches a realistic chance of success before expecting to intervene through the courts at all.

Agreements
The Children Act requires us to take a cautious, inter-agency approach, in which the LEA consults with other professionals, as well as with the parents and child, in order to attempt changes in the family's behaviour on a voluntary basis. Schools are vital partners in these programmes and many EWOs/ESWs will now be offering schools some kind of written agreement between all parties as a way of making progress (see figure 4.2).

These, unlike some 'contracts' which may be drawn up by a school, require give and take on *all* sides in order to make progress towards an achievable goal. They do not necessarily expect all the changes to be made by the child, or by their parents, nor necessarily

LEA's powers to respond to non-attendance at school, post-Children Act 1989	
work within voluntary framework	casework/groupwork alternatives to school
work within written agreements	special units etc home tuition/referral to other agencies programmes of action
s17(10) Children Act 1989 where child concerned may be defined as a child 'in need'	request LA to 'provide services' to child and family (Part III)
s27(4) Children Act 1989 where child has been assessed as having special educational needs	LA 'Should assist . . . with the provision of services'
s8/s10 Children Act 1989 where LEA may seek leave to apply for either a specific issue order or a prohibited steps order	orders may include specific directions that the parents take certain action or do not take certain actions (eg, admit a child to a school/not allow them to work in school hours)
s198 Education Act 1993 – school attendance order (child not registered at any school)	
s36 Children Act 1989 – education supervision order (Schedule 3 Part III) welfare checklist applies; child 'not being properly educated' (order must be better for child than no order)	supervisor to 'advise assist and befriend and may give directions' to child/parents
s199 Education Act 1993 – magistrates court prosecution – 'unauthorised absence'; (prosecution of parents for failing to follow reasonable directions under an ESO)	fines etc or may 'direct LEA to apply for ESO' (8 weeks) (imprisonment abolished)
s47(1)(b) Children Act 1989 where there is 'reasonable cause to suspect that a child is suffering, or is likely to suffer, significant harm' including harm to 'intellectual/social development'	child protection investigation by LA which could lead to child assessment order (s43) or emergency protection order (s44); CAO could include an assessment by educational psychologist
s31 Children Act 1989 – care proceedings by LA/supervision order to LA (caselaw has established that not attending school may fulfil 'significant harm' criterion)	'significant harm' + parental care not reasonable or child beyond parental control

Figure 4.1 *LEA powers*

County Council
Pride in your County
Education Welfare Section

(1)
(2)
(3)
(4)
(5)

Child's name: d.o.b.:
School:
Problem:

This agreement is intended to achieve the following:

(a)

(b)

(c)

What will be done by each party to this agreement? (as above):
(indicate timescales as appropriate – when will things be done?)

(1)

(2)

(3)

(4)

(5)

This agreement is intended to last until: _____

If anyone feels the agreement is not being kept they will

If this agreement breaks down the following action will be taken

Any further issues/arrangements: *(e.g. rewards for success)*

Arrangements for review:

Person responsible for review: Tel:

We consent to this agreement and understand what it means:

(1) name _____ signed _____
(2) name _____ signed _____
(3) name _____ signed _____
(4) name _____ signed _____
(5) name _____ signed _____

Date: _____

(Copies of this agreement will be made for each party)

Figure 4.2 *Written agreement*

to achieve the final result in one step. A child who is not attending at all may see three days a week as a possibility. If he is expected to reach full time, with full uniform, no behavioural problems and all his homework done right from day one, we are simply setting him up to fail. However, there is a growing body of experience which suggests that confronting parents and children with the problems in a process of formal consultation, and then expecting everyone involved to make realistic commitments towards resolving them, actually works where threats of court do not.

Good agreements are modest in their ambitions, with short-term goals which can be monitored and reviewed in the light of changes. We must never delude ourselves into thinking that such partnerships are equal; doing a deal with a school or even an LEA must feel to many parents like taking on a very powerful and distant giant – apparently friendly but capable of turning very nasty if the mood changes! Sometimes agreements will be presented as a last chance – 'co-operate or we'll take you to court', which is hardly a meeting of equals. But, sensitively done and using language that people can understand, they have a real place in solving problems.

The important thing is to seek to make them in ways which empower the parents, and even the child, rather than the authorities. They are the people with the responsibility in the situation. That may weigh heavily on them or they may give the impression that it means nothing. Either way our involvement is to encourage them to move forward, not to get bogged down in accusations and criticism or take decisions for them. Such an approach requires, of course, a willingness to try. It will not always be successful. Not all parents and children will want to change; not all schools will feel able to put in the effort, without which there can be no hope of improvement. Probably timing is everything but agreements made at the right time can and do work.

Care proceedings
While not going to school is no longer, in itself, grounds for care proceedings by the LEA, a very small minority of non-attenders, with whom agreement is impossible, might still end up 'in care' under the provisions of the Children Act, though 'accommodation' on a voluntary basis will be a much more frequent alternative. If, however, this is the best way of promoting their welfare and if, for example, absence from school is only one aspect of a whole network of behaviour which is causing the child 'significant harm' or putting him at risk of it, only a care order might offer sufficient authority to address his problem.

It was certainly wrong in the past that an LEA could make the application, albeit in consultation with the SSD, but then not have to carry out the order if made. But now other professionals must recognize that in these circumstances the power no longer lies with the LEA and that action, if needed, must be taken by the local authority, unless it has been established that the child has special *educational* needs which require residential provision to meet them.

Care proceedings will not necessarily resolve the child's non-attendance either; indeed it is increasingly unlikely given the very high threshold which must be reached before court action can be justified. The chances are that the child will already be excluded permanently or have developed such a lifestyle that school attendance is inconceivable. But they may provide an environment in which some alternative provision can become possible or offer the child some 'sanctuary' within which to begin rebuilding. Such proceedings may still provide the most appropriate way of enabling the child's whole circumstances to be addressed, including his education, taking account of the 'welfare checklist' and his complete range of needs.

Inter-agency tensions
Much of the impact of the Children Act should be in a change of style as much as any changes in the law. Schools and LEAs must work to the same map as other professionals and school staff in particular need to understand the profound impact which the Act has had on local authority social workers. They will not necessarily feel the need to 'do something' about the problem child. They are not faced with the daily repetition of their sense of failure which a nought in the register represents for teachers. They are often suspicious of schools, sometimes regarding them as repressive and unresponsive to the needs of children who don't easily fit in. Social workers work with individual clients and are concerned only with their best interests; teachers work with whole groups at once and are much more concerned about the impact this one individual has on all the others. These differing perceptions must be appreciated or there will be constant misunderstandings.

Social workers on the other hand need to recognize that educational professionals are caught in a variety of legislation, only some of which places the welfare of children at the centre. A teacher's primary task is to teach! School life is geared to success and conformity for the majority, and operates within an increasingly competitive environment. It is difficult for teachers to make exceptions for certain children, especially now that most schools are having to manage more children with fewer staff. Few schools are able to ignore their image and standing in the local community and so may be reluctant to persist with difficult children. But pastoral staff and social workers still have much in common – sometimes we are each an irritant on the hide of a massive beast; often neither of us can deliver what people ask of us. The Children Act should be where we meet, not where we fall apart.

Education (Pupils' Attendance Records) Regulations 1991

Authorized and unauthorized absence
These regulations became law just a few weeks before the Children Act, with little or no prior consultation with the education service. They have had a major impact on the way in which absence from school is perceived and dealt with. In addition to allowing schools to use computerized registration systems, these regulations require all schools to publish what the Government usually refers to as their 'truancy rate'. These are then compiled into league tables so that parents can compare one school with another.

It is the responsibility of the school to classify all absences as either 'authorized' or 'unauthorized', according to a standard coding system. This is not the parents' responsibility as many people seem to think. Teachers, children and parents have a right to clear procedures for making such decisions according to *whole school* policies which have been approved by governors. This decision presents no problem in many cases, but there are inevitably grey areas in which the absence of agreed criteria could easily lead to unfairness and confusion. But it may be a helpful way of identifying problems at an early stage, if handled carefully.

However, the publication of the figures is a different matter. There are already signs that the Secretary of State has recognised that his original expectations have proved wildly unrealistic. As there is no agreed definition of truancy, and as schools in practice have enormous discretion and control over how to classify any given absence, there is room for considerable variation in how these figures will eventually emerge. The league-tables of unauthorised absence published so far have clearly illustrated just how much depends on the criteria used. Some schools have claimed that they have none at all on the grounds that all absences have been accounted for, even if the explanations given are patently unacceptable. I have already come across 'she was drunk/hungover' and 'he was caught shoplifting' as grounds for authorizing an absence! (The regulations do say that only 'unavoidable' absences should be authorized.)

Other schools will be left with absences which they feel they cannot authorize simply because no explanation has been given, or because the tutor forgot to ensure a note was sent in. Some of these absences might have been for entirely justified reasons. Some schools will interpret the regulations very generously and exercise considerable creativity in accounting for the absences; others will want to send a clear signal to parents and children that unreasonable absences will not be excused and so end up with a much higher figure of unauthorized absence, even though the levels of *attendance* may be exactly the same. It could then be only the second school which is seen to have the 'truancy' problem even though it is the one which is doing something to stop it!

Understandably, headteachers are under considerable pressure, not least from their governors, to keep the rates of unauthorized absence as low as possible. Children who are seen as 'dragging down the school' will be at even greater risk of exclusion as a result. There is a very real danger that more effort will now go into presenting the figures than actually tackling the absences, especially as schools become increasingly self-confident in their own management. But any child who is having a great deal of time off school, for whatever reason, has a problem in keeping up with their education. There may appear to be no problem if all the absences have been accounted for.

Implications for prosecution of parents

The regulations were issued with a statement that the Government would like to see more 'early' prosecutions. Authorizing absences, however, certainly removes any power the LEA has to do so, as such children are now absent 'with leave', thus providing an immediate defence under the relevant section of the 1993 Act. Only unauthorized absences are evidence of any offence. But keeping them unauthorized is not normally thought to be in the school's best interests and teachers and governors are naturally keen to avoid accumulating rows of empty noughts. This then makes prosecution impossible. All this may make it difficult to put in the effort required to deal with the *causes* of the absenteeism as long as the league-table figure is acceptable. In the end, however, this strategy will surely prove only a short-term solution if the signal is sent that absence doesn't really matter much and that almost any explanation will do.

Of course not all schools work in this way, though there are major temptations to do so once levels of 'truancy' become part of the process by which a school will be evaluated. Presumably it will be a key indicator of a 'failing' school under the provisions of the 1993

Act, though there are surely ways of presenting the figures with explanations about what is being done in response to the absences or how many children are responsible for the vast bulk of them.

As with bullying and, to some extent, child protection, some schools may feel reluctant to acknowledge that this is a problem for them, for fear of what this will do to their reputation and status in the eyes of parents and the Government. But that leaves the children's needs unaddressed, their welfare unprotected. Alongside the difficult pressures caused by these regulations, many will want to give a clear welcome to the Children Act as a source of encouragement in making sure that the needs of some of the most vulnerable children in our society are not overlooked in the rush for respectability.

EDUCATION SUPERVISION ORDERS

A useful tool?

The new power under s36 of the Children Act to have a child of compulsory school age placed under the supervision of the LEA where they are 'not being properly educated', has met with a mixed reaction. Some LEAs have indicated that they do not intend to use it, or that they will apply only when directed to do so by a magistrates' court following an adult prosecution. Others appear to have been somewhat over-enthusiastic, submitting large numbers of inappropriate applications which have been largely unsuccessful. Yet others have seen this new power, in the context of the Act as a whole, as an opportunity to professionalize their welfare service by taking on a more 'social work oriented' way of working, while recognizing that the orders themselves are only suitable in a rather narrow range of situations.

All EWOs/ESWs have been helped both by Government guidance (Vol 7 – see Appendix 2) and by policy statements from the National Association of Social Workers in Education/Association of Chief Education Social Workers. These should ensure some consistency of practice and copies of each should be available to teachers locally on request.

Education supervision orders cannot be seen as a direct replacement for care proceedings under previous legislation. Many of the children for whom care orders were sought in the past will not be suitable for an ESO and may still need such a response. Care orders were never made *only* because the child was a poor school attender. But these new orders surely have their place, where education is the major focus of the problems, voluntary ways of working have broken down and there is still a realistic chance of improving the child's performance before they leave school. Both authorized and unauthorized absences can be the basis of the intervention and an order could also be sought with respect to children being educated 'otherwise than at school' where some failure to ensure it was being done properly had been established.

Seeking an order

Proceedings under the Children Act are not punitive. A child is not 'sentenced' to an education supervision order and language of this kind should not be used to describe it. An order does place both children and their parents under certain obligations to work with the supervisor and, if necessary, to follow their instructions. The supervisor is normally a suitably qualified EWO/ESW, responsible for establishing some external authority and support within the family, so that the child's educational needs may be more effectively met.

As elsewhere under the Act, children and parents must be fully consulted throughout and parents in particular should be regarded as partners with the supervisor wherever possible. A reasonably co-operative approach from parents is required as the aim of the order will be to strengthen and encourage them in exercising their responsibility towards the child rather than to take responsibility from them. However, there must be some element of disagreement and lack of progress by either parents or child to justify seeking an order at all. This will frequently be a fine judgement to make but some families need this structured support; some actually welcome it when it is done in the right way.

Education supervision orders can be applied for only by the LEA (for children in both LEA maintained and grant maintained schools), and the application is usually heard in the family proceedings court at magistrates' level. In some circumstances, for example where there are other proceedings in progress concerning the same child, it might be heard by a higher court but this will be rare. Prior consultation with the SSD *must* take place in order to establish that no other action would be more appropriate to promote the child's welfare. (There has been some confusion over the fact that the Act says consultation should be with the appropriate *Committee*, but delegation to officers would be the normal approach in other Children Act work. Now amended by schedule 19.149 Education Act 1993.)

Family proceedings

Family proceedings courts are new courts established with the Children Act, staffed by specially trained magistrates from the family panel. Criminal matters involving children and people under 18 are now heard in the youth court under entirely different procedures and different legislation. The two kinds of proceedings should not be confused, though school pastoral staff may be called upon to supply information or reports for either. The juvenile court has been abolished. Family proceedings courts can deal with a whole range of 'public' and 'private' law applications, though many issues in connection with divorce and separation will continue to be dealt with through family proceedings at county divorce courts.

The application procedure is complex and time-consuming, not least because of the importance of ensuring that everyone involved is kept fully informed throughout. All court work under the Children Act involves an immense amount of paperwork as all information and evidence has to be disclosed in writing in advance and then circulated to all the relevant parties. In normal circumstances, all those with parental responsibility, *together with the child concerned*, are 'parties' in the proceedings (respondents), along with the LEA (applicant). There is a fee for making an application (currently £50 for each child), and most of the business is conducted through solicitors. Other people who are not automatically parties, such as step-parents or unmarried fathers, may apply to be joined or may be joined at the request of others. It is not normal for a guardian *ad litem* to be appointed in ESO applications.

Court hearings

In most cases there will first be a 'directions appointment' in which all the parties meet with the clerk of the court to go through the evidence and establish whether there are any issues which may prove controversial or which need clarification. Further information may be called for or time allowed for written evidence to be filed and responded to. But the general emphasis on avoiding delay in Children Act matters should mean that a final hearing should be reached within a few weeks at the most. It is possible (as happened in one of the first applications I made) that the directions appointment may be held before the main court session, with the final hearing then fixed for later in the morning! There is no absolute requirement to have a directions appointment, though I am not sure that this is good practice. Magistrates' clerks, however, have considerable discretion.

The court hearings are relatively informal, though to a parent and a child they must still seem fairly intimidating. The only decision to be made is whether or not to grant the order, unless there are also other issues (eg, concerning residence) to be decided at the same time. If the court is not satisfied that the application is appropriate, it may call for more information or direct the SSD to carry out an investigation of the child's circumstances.

Action plans

The basis on which an order will be made is that the LEA is able to demonstrate to the court that it will be of positive benefit to the child. The magistrates will not necessarily grant the order just because they have been asked to do so, even if the child has a poor record of attendance. The application must contain an action plan which sets out what the LEA intends to do and why the order will help in achieving it. As with all orders under the Act, an ESO does not provide *carte blanche* – the court must be satisfied that the order is better for the child than no order, so it must know what will happen afterwards.

In most situations the action plan will only set out what has been the preferred package of action all along but which has not been successful by voluntary means. It may propose changes which could only be made with the authority which the order would give, including even a change of school. It is then for the court to determine whether what is proposed is in the child's best interests and, in effect, to order that the child/parents co-operate rather than simply relying on their agreement. This whole process requires considerable social work skill if it is to be effective.

The role of schools

Schools are clearly a crucial part of ensuring the success of any order where the child is a registered pupil, even though school staff are not actually party to the proceedings. Full consultation with key staff should take place in advance, especially over the contribution which they will make to the action plan. School reports are essential (though the Government's guidance sees them only as 'helpful'), setting out in particular the child's academic progress and the educational opportunity which is being put at risk by the absence (see figure 4.3).

It is interesting to note that the role of the school was greatly enhanced between the first version of the guidance and that which was eventually published. This clearly reflects more accurately the

SCHOOL REPORT

EDUCATION SUPERVISION ORDER – application with respect to:

Child's Name: _____ d.o.b. _____

Address: _____

School: _____ Year Group: _____

Please complete the following questions making sure that, wherever possible, comments are factual rather than opinion.

1. ATTAINMENT (Please indicate this pupil's current level of achievement, results of assessments etc. and general level of ability. Indicate strengths as well as weaknesses and any provision for special educational needs.)

2. EFFECT OF ABSENCE (Please indicate what has been missed due to this pupil's absences and the effect this would have on their educational progress/achievement)

3. FUTURE PROSPECTS What could this pupil hope to achieve if they attended regularly?

4. EDUCATION SUPERVISION ORDER (Please indicate your attitude to this application, your role in prior consultation and the part which will be played by the school in encouraging its success.)

5. ANY FURTHER COMMENTS

I believe this information is true and understand that it may be placed before the Court:

Signed: _____ Name: _____ Designation: _____
Date: _____

Figure 4.3 *School report*

considerable responsibility which a school must carry in ensuring the order's success and the degree of consultation to which it is therefore entitled. There is a danger that school staff will not feel any great sense of commitment to what the LEA is doing unless they have an opportunity to be involved throughout. Without that support the order is doomed from the start.

Sanctions

Education supervision orders contain limited sanctions if they are not proving successful. The supervisor has a general duty to 'advise, assist and befriend' but also has the power to issue written 'directions' to the child or their parents, specifying action which must be taken. This could include attending a meeting, following instructions from school staff etc. The supervisor has a duty to take the child's/parents' wishes into account when issuing such directions, and to issue them only when all else has failed.

Persistent failure by parents to follow these directions is an offence on the same scale as failure to ensure regular attendance. If it is the child who is persistently failing, the supervisor must consult with the SSD which *must* then investigate the child's circumstances. It will then determine whether other action, including care proceedings, should be considered. The order can be discharged early on the application of either the LEA, the parents or the child.

In reality, 'casework' ways of working, or the imaginative use of groupwork and educational alternatives, are more likely to be effective than relying on threats of further action. Orders are normally only appropriate when the child has long enough left at school to make them worthwhile – they are *not* the panacea with which to address the difficulties of disaffected pupils in the final few months of year 11. They may be of particular value in assisting a child through a period of transition, especially from year 6 to year 7 or from year 9 to year 10. Children who are missing out at this point are at risk of causing themselves considerable difficulty for the rest of their school career. The sustained support of an order at this point may enable them and their parents to ensure that they have gained every possible advantage from the choices they have to make at these times.

Monitoring and review

An order will be subject to regular review, at which all those involved must be given full opportunity to express the need for any changes. Crises will be best dealt with here rather than by unilateral action by anyone: LEA, school, parent or child. Orders can be extended beyond the original year but this is likely to be very uncommon. Children may, in exceptional circumstances, be subject to both an ESO to the LEA and a supervision order to the SSD, but an order cannot be made on a child who is already on a care order and the making of a care order discharges any ESO. An order could, however, be made on a child who is being 'accommodated'.

Education supervision orders will not be a common occurrence, even in those LEAs which have received them with some enthusiasm, but they do represent an interesting opportunity to address the needs of a few children. Time will tell how effective they will be.

PROMOTING BETTER ATTENDANCE

Whole school policy

The Government has made it clear that promoting good attendance is a key task facing schools for the future. The White Paper 'Choice and Diversity' which preceded the 1993 Act, recognized that there is little point in reforming the curriculum if children are not there to benefit from it. The Act itself re-states parents' statutory duties in this area though it contains no new initiatives for tackling the problems. There is no hard and fast evidence about how widespread unauthorized absence from school really is, but clearly a percentage of children do not readily fit in with the normal expectations which most never question to any significant extent. Others are given explicit or tacit support by parents in staying away from school either occasionally or more frequently.

A school which is seeking to promote the welfare of children will want to have a positive policy on promoting better attendance. It is easy to take this issue for granted, especially in schools which do not feel they have a serious problem, but even if there are only a few children who need help there should be a strategy in place for making sure they get it. Children respond best when they feel that their needs are being met. This is not always easy in a climate of high unemployment where many young people feel that there is not much point in bothering with education.

It is a remarkable compliment to their teachers that so many children do come to school so regularly in view of some of the other role models around them and the sense of despair and hopelessness which pervades many communities. But some children have genuine difficulty handling the school environment and any policy to deal with non-attenders must be sensitive enough to differentiate between children with behavioural problems or anxieties, phobias and learning difficulties, those whose family life is undergoing serious disruption, those burdened by domestic responsibilities including the care of young children or elderly relatives and those struggling with a deep-seated cultural perception that school is not for the likes of them. All these are genuine reasons why a child may find coming to school difficult, though the responses required may be very different.

The needs of the individual

A welfare approach to bringing about improvements in attendance will recognize the complexity of children's lives and seek to be as accommodating to their needs as possible. It is not simply a question of trying to ensure marks in registers but a genuine attempt to appreciate the child's difficulties. Of course, children cannot have things all their own way, but the greater the part they have played in helping us to understand their behaviour the more likely they are to 'own' the outcome. Individual targets which make use of the headteacher's power to disapply the requirements of the national curriculum for a temporary period, or more modest expectations than those which normally apply, are more likely to bring about improvements than offering children only impossible mountains to climb.

Much absence from school is habitual, like many things in life. Children learn to stay away, not always enjoying it very much but finding it hard to break the habit. Their behaviour will need relearning with positive reinforcements and, above all, a sense that someone is actually interested in them as a person and in whether or not they attend. Teachers should not, however, feel that they have to face such problems alone. Much of this work will be done in part-nership – with EWOs/ESWs, with other professionals such as educational psychologists and Child and Family Services and, vitally, with parents. Sadly, many families are intimidated by schools; their own experiences of education were often far from positive and they do not feel able to work with teachers on equal terms. Much non-cooperation by parents is actually based on a lack of experience; just not knowing what to do for the best. To overcome this, the principles of the Children Act about consultation and agreement have to be made explicit, not taken as read.

Using the welfare checklist

One way of doing this is once again to make use of s1(3). This provides a framework within which consultation could take place and could ensure some kind of consistency in assessing appropriate responses to individual children's poor school attendance. Ideally this process should be shared directly with the child and their parents, along with any other persons who may be significant in seeking to meet the child's needs. Most of it is simply common sense, but unless we have distanced ourselves from what we are doing and evaluated it in some way, there is always the risk of making inaccurate assumptions about a particular child's absence.

What are the wishes and feelings of the child?
It is essential that the child concerned is given an opportunity to be heard within the process. This could be done in a number of ways – preferably not just by putting him on the spot in a room full of adults and saying 'What do you intend to do about it then?' Perhaps time could be spent with the child alone before any meeting or one of the adults involved could have the special responsibility of getting to know the problem from the child's perspective. I have certainly known examples where the resolution of the problem became obvious once the young person was heard. A child may often say nothing when asked to explain his absence; he may not actually have an explanation to offer. It may take time to tease out what he is feeling. It may be necessary to use diagrams and pictures to help him express himself. There are a number of exercises and activities available such as drawing a chart depicting life's vital milestones or making a personal shield which expresses matters of greatest importance. It is vital that the child feels that he is being heard, even if others want to challenge his version of events or even if, in the end, he cannot have things exactly the way he wants them.

What are the child's needs?
This should be more than a matter of personal opinion. Wherever possible, objective assessments should be available or, if they are needed, obtained from those who may be able to help. Does the child have special educational needs which have never been properly assessed or is referral to some specialist support service required? Would some groupwork be helpful to him? What is available? Does he need some alternative educational provision? It will be important to set the child's educational needs within the context of his overall needs as a person. There might, for example, be issues within the child's family where he feels his needs are not being met – for more contact with a parent or for the resolution of some dispute about his care perhaps. There may be practical pro-

blems to do with space at home or lack of attention from his parents. He may be feeling confused about himself as a person or lacking in confidence in making and keeping friends. What resources are available within the school, and beyond, to enable the child to address his needs more effectively? What skills might he need to acquire and who can teach them?

What would be the effect of any change in his circumstances?
This will be of particular significance if the child is close to exclusion or court proceedings are being considered. Attention must always be paid to the likely effects of any major changes in the child's life. Should a change of school be considered, or a change of tutor group or timetable? If the child did change his non-attending behaviour, what effects might this have, for example on his role in the family? Some children feel guilty about going to school and leaving a sick parent. Might there be powerful incentives operating to prevent him changing his behaviour and if so, what can be done about them? Particular attention might need to be paid to how the school will receive the child if he does attend. Many children tell stories of being made to feel unwelcome or ridiculed because they have changed their behaviour from absence to attendance. What problems might be caused for the child if he did change as people are asking him to? What rewards might operate; how might other areas of his life be affected? Above all, what vision can the school offer as to what his life could be like with improved attendance? Children need to know what they are aiming for, not simply be expected to do as they are told.

What characteristics of the child are relevant?
This provides an opportunity to see the child as an individual; to understand his behaviour as unique to him rather than assuming that he is simply acting typically. Are issues of race, culture, gender, disability, or sexuality important? What kind of person is he – what are his strengths and weaknesses, what does he enjoy and hate about his life, his family, the school? It is difficult for schools to think in terms of individuals. Children are classified by year groups or ability ranges. But each child is, of course, unique. This may be another area where it helps to make use of non-verbal ways of enabling the child to express himself. How does he see himself? What does he see as important or does he feel inadequate, tired of people telling him that he is of no value? Of particular importance is trying to understand how *this* child feels about his absence from school. There is a common assumption that all children who miss

school are roaming the streets getting into trouble or lying in bed all day enjoying their idleness. In fact, he may be afraid, or depressed, or lonely, but unable to break out of the spiral. How has he coped with the absence and what does that say about his individual character and personality?

What harm is he at risk of suffering?
The aim is always to seek to ensure this child's welfare and protect him from harm. He may not feel that he is coming to any harm by not attending school. If that is the assessment of everyone else as well then some positive alternative goal is needed because that is all there is to work on. But many children do suffer through non-attendance, not only academically, but socially. Some become withdrawn while others are overtly acting-out to such an extent that they may be running risks with sex, alcohol, drugs, petty crime or gambling. Such children probably need far more than simply a return to school. This analysis may even reveal that not going to school is the least of his problems at the moment and perhaps it is better to concentrate on other things in order to enable him to reduce the other risks he is running. It will often be a key objective of this process to help a child to see that he is the only loser by his behaviour and that there is a genuine alternative on offer. If the primary damage is educational, what strategies might be available to rebuild some of that which has been missed? Are there crucial parts of the school career ahead, like choosing options, which set a deadline by which progress must be made if even more harm is not to be done? How could that point be reached in a more managed way to minimize the damage?

How capable are the child's parents of meeting his needs?
This needs to be approached with caution as there is little point in giving parents the impression that they have been consulted only so that they can be blamed for what has gone wrong. Parents *are* sometimes responsible for their child's absence from school; they may be totally unable to appreciate how the child is reacting to some problem in their own relationship or they may have abandoned responsibility altogether. They may be rewarding the child for not going to school, in either overt or subtle ways. But they may simply lack the basic parenting skills that the child needs if he is to thrive. If there are financial or housing pressures, or competing demands from other children, or if parents simply cannot handle the child, there is little point in blaming them. The Children Act says that parents are entitled to support in bringing up their children. What support do these parents need? What unmet needs do *they* have

which, if addressed, would increase their competence and understanding? What skills do they need to learn in order to be able to correct the child's non-attendance, such as how to apply appropriate rewards and sanctions? Who will help them? In particular, what can the school do to build new relationships with the parents and what special arrangements for home–school liaison might be needed in order to encourage them?

Are court orders now appropriate?
Has the time come for consideration to be given to whether either prosecution of parents or some order under the Children Act is now required – under either private or public law? Have all possible means of resolving the problems on a voluntary basis been exhausted? If action in the courts may now be needed, which agency has the responsibility for acting? What consultation procedures are now appropriate? It may be that parents or others should be encouraged to initiate applications under private law themselves rather than assuming that an agency should act. The test here is whether it can be demonstrated that an order would be of positive benefit to the child. What commitments might the school need to make to ensure the success of such applications?

Of course all this is very time-consuming and there are no guarantees of success. Much of this could be the responsibility of an EWO/ESW to manage rather than a teacher. But children will not change their behaviour unless everyone works together. Such a model at least provides a framework within which to try.

CASE STUDIES

As with the studies about parental responsibility, what follows should not be taken too literally, but does provide an indication of the kind of intervention which may be appropriate in response to individual children's absence from school. The studies are again based on real examples with the names changed and each has a title which identifies its main theme.

Evidence for prosecution

Tony has been attending less than half the time since the beginning of term, usually missing six or seven days at a time. His mother always sends him back to school with notes to explain his absences so they have all been authorized, but he seems to have more than his fair share of stomach upsets! Other children in his class say that they have seen him out playing on their way home from school and that he seems fine. Tony's mother isn't on the phone and hasn't been to the school for some years. She doesn't answer letters which are sent home. The school refers to their EWO who makes home visits when Tony is off school. It is clear that he is able to obtain a note whenever he wishes and that his mother enjoys having him at home during the day to keep her company. A written agreement should be attempted, setting out the rules by which the school will authorize Tony's absences in future. They will only be authorized after the first two days if Tony is referred to a GP and his mother agrees that the school nurse can check each time he is absent. The absences which are then left unauthorized could be used as evidence for a prosecution if the agreement fails.

Written agreements

Jane has been absent for several weeks and the EWO can never find anyone in the house during the day. Jane is still living there as other children have seen her, but neither letters nor phone calls have brought any response. The education department puts its absence procedures into effect and arranges a formal consultation meeting to include Jane, her mother and her father who is divorced from her mother and lives a few miles away. The first time, Jane's mother rings just before the meeting to say she can't come. A second meeting is arranged two days later to which everyone comes. Jane is very quiet but eventually it emerges that she is baby-sitting for her older sister or just staying in the house listening to music. She says she doesn't like school as everyone says she is fat. Her mother claims she hadn't realized how many weeks had gone by but also admits that she should have acted sooner. Her father didn't know there was any problem and now says he will take more interest and keep in contact with the school. The school is prepared to allow Jane to return gradually and an appointment is made for her to meet the teacher who runs a girls' group one lunchtime a week. A written agreement sets out all the arrangements, to be reviewed every two weeks so that Jane's attendance can be gradually increased. Her mother agrees to try and change her working hours so that she is there in the early mornings. The absences on Jane's 'leave' days will be authorized as long as she attends on the others.

Inter-agency co-operation

Brian and Sharon have always been poor attenders. The EWO has been a frequent visitor to the house and things improve after regular reminders and help with transporting the children to school in the morning. They have two younger brothers under school age, one of whom has mild cerebral palsy. They are often needed to help with the domestic routine, especially in the mornings. Various support services have been made available to the family but the EWO is becoming increasingly concerned. The school is tolerant of their situation but staff are beginning to ask if they can authorize at least some of the absences. The two children account for nearly half the absences in their year and the headteacher is afraid of the effect that leaving them unauthorized may have on the school's league-table position. The LEA is reluctant to consider court action as any fine would only increase the pressure on their parents who are already deep in debt. The education department invokes its absence from school procedures and invites all agencies, and the family, to a consultation meeting. Each agency is asked to co-operate in drawing up a plan. For the first time, Brian and Sharon's mother admits that she often can't cope and that perhaps she needs a break from at least some of the children. Perhaps 'accommodation' might help to ease the problems for a while, during which time a proper inter-agency response could be drawn up with the parents. School attendance is only part of a much wider range of issues to be addressed by everyone working together.

Education supervision orders

Amjad and his family made a written agreement with the school six weeks ago in order to tackle his regular absences. The agreement hasn't been very successful and he continues to miss at least two days every week. It seems he sets off for school most days but sometimes never arrives. He often returns home but has recently started hanging around in the local park instead. His parents had considered taking away his door-key but this is problematic as they sometimes arrive home late. Amjad admits that the absences are his fault, and can't really explain them, although he finds school boring and says that the teachers don't like him, especially his year head. This is a crucial year for him as he needs to make his options choices for his GCSEs and he is getting seriously behind, even in those subjects which he says he likes. His school is willing to consider a change of pastoral tutor but only if he attends more regularly first. His parents have always said that they supported the efforts of the EWO and the school but they feel they are losing control over him and that they have many other pressing commitments outside the home. In general, Amjad is an ordinary enough lad but his parents feel increasingly frustrated about his attitude to school. If no further progress can be made by agreement, an education supervision order might be considered, in order to give Amjad and his family a structured programme within which to work and to encourage his parents to be consistent in addressing his needs. It may be that some shared arrangement between the school and a support unit may be available, which the order would require Amjad to attend. Other professionals may be needed, including an assessment of any special educational needs or emotional problems.

School refusal

Janet hasn't been to school for eight weeks. The EWO is aware that Social Services have been involved, though there has never been a formal inter-agency meeting. It appears that she has been sexually active for some months and is spending a lot of time with her older boyfriend, who left school last year. It is rumoured at the school that she has had an abortion, but the family have wanted to keep her problems confidential and so no one seems entirely clear as to what is going on. Janet was referred to a Child and Family Psychiatric Service for help but has refused to keep appointments. She has made no complaint against the boy concerned and so no criminal proceedings are planned. Her parents say that they can cope and that she will come back to school in her own good time. Within the limits of reasonable confidentiality, further inter-agency consultation must take place to determine who is going to address Janet's needs. Are child protection issues significant? Who can win Janet's confidence and help her to express her wishes and feelings? Should a short-term alternative to mainstream school be offered, or should Janet's parents be required to ensure her return, albeit gradually? Home tuition may offer a temporary solution but the school believes she is capable of high achievement in her final two years with regular attendance. The boundaries of a new plan, to be attempted first by agreement, must be determined as a matter of some urgency. If no other agency is planning any action and no agreement is forthcoming, an ESO might give Janet more effective supervision and the protection of a formal programme of help, if the court agreed that this was in her interests.

Listening to children

Claire's parents have lost the final stages of appeal over their choice of secondary school for her. The school of their choice is heavily over-subscribed but they have refused to admit her to any other school until the dispute is sorted out. They have consistently said that they will not send her anywhere if they cannot choose which school she goes to. During the appeals period they are given the benefit of the doubt, even though this means her missing several weeks at school, but, having lost the final appeal, the EWO informs them that they must now either choose an alternative school, or indicate, in writing, that they intend to educate her 'otherwise'. No such letter is forthcoming, so the initial stages of a school attendance order are considered. Claire and her parents are invited to a formal meeting to discuss the options and, in the end, an agreement is reached which enables her to be admitted elsewhere. Claire's parents are advised that her attendance will be closely monitored and that any unauthorized absences may be used as the basis of a prosecution. Interestingly, during a subsequent home visit, Claire confides to the EWO that *she* never wanted to go to the other school anyway but her parents took no notice.

5

Power to the Pupils?

CHILDREN'S RIGHTS AND THE CHILDREN ACT

A new view of children

Any review of the significance of the Children Act would be incomplete without recognizing that one of its aims is to encourage children to participate more fully in decisions which affect their lives. When the Government is asked about its commitment to the United Nations Convention on the Rights of the Child (ratified by the UK in December 1991), ministers usually point to the Children Act as evidence that they are taking this issue seriously and seeking to empower children through the legislative process. Whether the Act actually does what was being asked for is not the concern of this chapter, though it could be argued that any serious attempt to give children a better deal should include not just the rather domestic issues of the Children Act but wider, more structural issues such as poverty and housing.

The point is that the Act is clearly intended to change our usual perspective. Children are now seen in a very different way than under most previous legislation. They are no longer simply the recipients of other people's decisions about what may be in their best interests, but active partners in determining what should happen to them. The Act finally removes any suggestion that children are simply part of their parents' property – to be disposed of like houses or furniture when their parents divorce or separate. As the Convention also makes clear, they are individuals in their own right; their view on their life is as valid as anyone else's.

There are a number of points in the Act where this is clear and others where it may be implied:

A right to be consulted

The 'welfare checklist' puts children's wishes and feelings as the first item to be considered when some issue about their welfare has arisen. Not that this means that it is the most important, nor that what the child wants or feels will necessarily be the course of action that results. But children must be asked; they have a right to be heard and should be given the opportunity to express themselves before important decisions are made. This is clearly in line with the Convention.

There have been examples where orders have been made, such as an order determining where the child should live, which have subsequently been overturned on appeal because the original decision did not adequately take the child's wishes and feelings into account. (Another example concerned a dispute over which school a child should attend where the order was set aside because the child was not asked for his views.) The DoH has produced a range of special leaflets for children and young people which explain their rights under the Act (see Appendix 2). Although they may not be widely recognized outside the care system, court welfare officers, social workers and others are responsible for ensuring that such rights are respected.

Independent application

Children who can convince the court that they are competent can initiate their own applications for orders under the Act in order to resolve some issue to do with their welfare. A child may feel they are being deprived of sufficient contact with a grandparent or that they wish to see their father even though their mother does not approve. They may even raise the issue of where they will live, though this is uncommon. Solicitors who are familiar with family law issues have specific guidance available to assist them in representing children and helping them to make applications where appropriate. Where children are a party to the proceedings they have a right to their own solicitor to speak for them, independently of whoever is representing their parents.

Participation

Children who are the subject of public law proceedings are usually involved in meetings and consultations to discuss what is going to happen to them. Clearly this is likely to be a more meaningful experience the older the child or young person is, but even quite young children may be offered ways of expressing their point of view even if participating in a formal meeting is not appropriate.

Guardians ad litem will also be responsible for ensuring that their best interests are served and that they understand everything which is happening.

'Gillick competency'

Children and young people have a right to refuse to be medically examined in connection with applications for certain orders, though this is less clear since the Court of Appeal judgement in 1992 which overturned a young person's refusal to receive treatment in life-threatening situations. However, the ruling of the House of Lords in 1985 in the case brought by Victoria Gillick against West Norfolk and Wisbech Area Health Authority, has clearly established that a child of 'sufficient understanding and intelligence' has the power to give consent to medical treatment, including contraception, *in their own right* without need for parental permission.

This can prove an awkward issue for schools to handle, if the child requires time away from school for treatment and advice and does not wish their parents to be informed. In general, unless a child protection issue is raised, they would have a reasonable right to such confidentiality. Any such absences which *must* be during the day, for example, asking for the 'morning after' pill, could be authorized on medical grounds, though this must be a matter for individual discretion by headteachers.

Complaints

Children being looked after by the local authority have a right to make complaints about a wide range of aspects of their care. Volume 4 of the Government's Children Act guidance devotes a whole chapter to the procedures which must be in place to enable service 'users', including children, to make representations about the quality of their care. The child is a central focus of these procedures, not simply added on as an afterthought. Any complaint which is submitted by someone else about a child's care must be checked out with him first to ensure that it adequately reflects his views. The procedures must be publicized and, crucially, must contain an *independent* element rather than simply being dealt with internally. Some children may also need 'independent visitors' to safeguard their interests and the wishes of the child about who they should be must be respected. A visitor cannot be appointed if the child objects to them.

Accommodation

Young people who are 16 or over may ask to be accommodated by the local authority in their own right, even against the wishes of their parents, or refuse their attempts to place them elsewhere. Even before that age the child's wishes about the arrangements being made by their parents must be sought and due attention paid to them. Children have a right to be heard in determining where they are placed, especially if racial, religious, cultural or linguistic issues are important. Children cannot be held in secure accommodation unless specific conditions apply and appropriate orders have been obtained. In any review of the circumstances of a child who is being looked after by the local authority, the child's views must be included and he must be kept fully informed of any proposed changes.

Pastoral care and the older child

In addition to these specific rights, there are other more subtle issues arising from the general philosophy of the Act which have wide-ranging implications. Anyone who has been involved in the pastoral care of teenagers will surely have come across a difficult tension. Young people are required to stay on at school until the Easter or the May of their final year. (This is likely to be even later under proposed changes.) Many year 11 pupils are by then well past their 16th birthday; legally entitled to be sexually active; able to leave home with their parents' permission (and probably without it in practice), old enough even to marry with the consent of those with parental responsibility for them – yet still not old enough to leave school. There was a famous case of a year 11 pupil who was asked to bring a note to explain her absence. A note from her husband would not be acceptable – it has to be from a parent!

Section 8 orders normally end on the child's 16th birthday, as if this is when parental responsibility ends, yet the Act defines a child as anyone under 18. There is some recognition in the Children Act guidance that things inevitably change when we are talking about 16–18-year-olds but this differential in society's expectations causes many problems – on the one hand old enough to be treated as a maturing young adult, on the other still required to be kept in a dependent relationship, forbidden by law from striking out alone and taking full responsibility for their own life. This, of course, is reinforced by the extreme difficulty facing young people who cannot live at home or who wish to be financially independent at a time when neither employment nor training may be available to them. Many choose further education at school which may exacerbate the ambiguity even further.

The 'mature minor'

The Children Act, and the *Gillick* ruling, have further sharpened this issue by accepting that 'children' have ever-increasing rights to take up views independent from those of their parents and by encouraging the concept of the 'mature minor'. It should be commonplace in any pastoral situation involving, for example, a 15-year-old girl who is sexually active, to consider whether or not she is 'suffering, or at risk of, significant harm' before any response to her behaviour is made.

Just because what she is doing is technically illegal (though *she* is not committing any offence), even if her parents do not approve, or do not even know, that in itself need not be sufficient for any agency to feel that they must intervene or for teachers to feel that they must contact parents. The concept of 'moral danger' no longer gives any basis for care proceedings. She may be taking sensible precautions, not only in terms of contraception but also by not putting herself at risk of sexual assault by persons other than her partner. She may be continuing to attend school and generally keeping her life well ordered. In this kind of situation she is likely to be given the right to make these decisions for herself and offered health care and advice without much fuss.

This does not necessarily mean, however, that no issues of child protection, parental responsibility or school attendance may arise. What about the rights of those who have parental responsibility for her until she is 18? That may appear to strengthen their claim to authority. If she is also refusing to attend school then some action may well be appropriate. There may be particular concerns about whether her consent is truly 'informed', especially if her partner is much older than she is – and what if she were 14, or 13? These questions could all need addressing and some attempt made to strike a balance between the various ideologies. But they are clearly competing and pastoral and welfare professionals are increasingly having to develop skills in determining what is the most appropriate course of action bearing in mind a variety of complex inter-relationships.

In making those decisions, the rights and views of the young person concerned will be crucial and should be taken very seriously. Even if we think they are wrong, we may have no power to overrule them. How do you *make* a 15 or 16-year-old act responsibly? There are few clearly accepted procedures and criteria which will be able to resolve the dilemmas for us. But for all the complication involved, the law now recognizes that we are not dealing with mindless infants or 'objects of concern', but maturing individuals with insights and perceptions of their own, even if they may not always act in their own best interests in the judgement of others. The Children Act is central to the strengthening of this position and school staff will often be caught in complex situations where children and their parents are in conflict. It cannot be assumed that the parents' or the school's wishes should always be upheld.

Other rights

And, of course, children have rights and duties in various other parts of their lives as well. Once they are 13 they can get a part-time job as long as it does not conflict with school time or put them at unreasonable risk. They can be left in charge of other people's children virtually at any age, but certainly from 13, with all the responsibilities which that entails. They can have their own bank account in their own name and from 10 onwards can be held accountable for offences which they commit.

Children can legally possess and use a firearm (under supervision) from 14 and drink alcohol in their own homes from the age of five! They can ask to see personal files held on them by an SSD or a doctor, if of an age to understand them. Children may be called at any age to give evidence as a witness in a court of law. At 15 they can legally see films which some would regard as seriously disturbing. But when it comes to school they have virtually no rights at all, except perhaps the right to education itself, and that is increasingly being withdrawn for many of those who need it most.

TAKING PUPILS SERIOUSLY

Whose education is it anyway?

When it comes to education, all the rights and powers rest with the parents, the school and, increasingly, with the Government. Not one of the reforms of education in the last decade has given any more statutory rights to the pupils, so far as I am aware. Of course education is supposed to be all about pupils. But in terms of rights, it is all about adults.

A publicity booklet published by the DfE outlining the achievements of grant maintained schools contains the views of all interested parties – except children. Governors, parents, the Secretary of State, teachers, employers; the list of those entitled to have a say appears endless. These are the people whose needs appear to be the focus of our education system, and it has probably been much the same in most systems which have come and gone during various shades of political opinion.

The UN Convention, Article 12, says that children have a right to express their views in *all* matters which affect their lives. Surely a right to have a say about their education must be a central aspect of any claim that such principles are being observed? Yet in Britain there is no statutory duty on anyone to ensure that they get it.

Speaking for children

Of course giving more say to parents is intended to enable them to act responsibly for the sake of their children. That is in line with the spirit of the Children Act. But there are two obvious problems with that argument:

(a) Most parents wouldn't deny that it is *their* children whose interests are uppermost in their minds. Few of us would admit to much sense of altruism in the exercise of our parental power. We are seeking the best for our children – who would blame us? But does that deliver an educational system which is in the interests of *all* children? That seems to be placing a rather heavy burden on the shoulders of individual parents who cannot be expected to take responsibility for the whole system. It will serve the needs of many, if not most, parents quite adequately; hopefully it will also deliver what is best for their children too. But what about the parents who cannot assert themselves; those whose children are not welcome; those who are uncomfortable with professionals and intimidated by them; those who will gain the school no status? Who will look to the needs of children whose parents will not or cannot do so, or whose needs are high on no one else's agenda?

b) Do parents actually understand their children's needs that well anyway, especially in our kind of society in which many families are experiencing the turmoil of broken relationships and when the pace of change is almost unbearable? Does any of us really know what it's like to be 14, or 10, or six today? How can *we* speak for our children – wouldn't it be so much better if we enabled them to speak for themselves?

Of course many parents do engage in open and honest discussion about important things in their child's life and give them opportunity to express their point of view. Some, however, do not. Children are often able to exploit their own situation and find ways of manipulating the rest of us; but sometimes they choose unwise ways to do it because more creative and considered ways are not available. Sometimes they choose any behaviour which will get them noticed because what they think and feel is not being recognized. Sometimes they are the last to know what's going on. And then, unsurprisingly, we find it hard to win their co-operation and they feel little sense of commitment to what others have determined is best for them.

Exploding the myth

I am not saying that children and young people should always have what they want. Far from it – in schools or anywhere else. All of us need boundaries and children in particular need to know where they stand and what the rules are. But it is foolish to assume that they will simply accept those boundaries because someone else has told them that they must. There is no longer an automatic acceptance by children that the teacher is always right. Perhaps too many children have discovered that adults are not to be trusted; they are unreliable, make mistakes, say one thing and then do another. Why should teachers be any different?

Hierarchical models of authority might have worked in previous generations when the social structure was more stable, or children may have fallen in line for fear of the consequences. But the Emperor has no clothes now and children know it. There are no punitive sanctions of any great significance in schools any more and there is no prospect of them returning, despite the cries of some for greater use of courts or the reintroduction of physical punishments.

It is inconceivable that teachers will ever again be allowed to hit the pupils in their care as a way of strengthening their authority – if you doubt this, just ask any 10-year-old and you will see how outrageous the very idea is. Such an approach flies in the face of all the child protection legislation and educational professionals would simply be marginalizing themselves from all other agencies were such practices accepted. Even exclusion may only offer the child what they wanted all along and contains little fear for those most likely to experience it.

The system can no longer operate on the basis of *imposed* authority because there is just no power to make it stick. The myth has been blown apart; the bluff called for ever. Yet still teachers are being asked to do the impossible, here as elsewhere. Every other influence on the growing child is encouraging them to be 'adults in the making'; to make choices, to take control – of their bodies, their relationships, their future, etc. Society wants freedom and choice everywhere else, but still expects schools to teach children to conform and to punish them when they don't. No wonder teachers often feel that they're losing their grip – this model of the teacher/ pupil relationship simply doesn't work any more.

Customer care

Instead of just bemoaning this situation, as some are tempted to do, or looking back to a golden age that probably never was, there has to be another way of doing things – a way which wins children over and gains their respect because they too can see the sense of it. Surely educationalists of all people should believe in such a possibility? Neither parents nor teachers will be respected simply for their status. Commitment from children will not be achieved in schools unless, as the Children Act requires professionals and parents to do in other contexts, they are given a voice and notice is taken of what they say. It is time that education started to think about its 'customer care'.

As always under the Children Act, there are issues to do with 'age and understanding' here. Most of these issues are especially relevant for secondary schools. But a child of 10 is considered old enough to take responsibility for his own behaviour if caught shoplifting. Why is he not usually considered old enough to be an active participant in helping to run his school or influence its policy? Giving children more power will be open to abuse, just as it is when all the power is concentrated in the hands of adults. But how will children learn to exercise power responsibly if they are never given opportunities to do so within the education system?

There is something increasingly old-fashioned about the idea that children are required only to be the recipients of education; that they are needed only to turn up and absorb what others have put in place for them. Are they not entitled to more than that? Don't they need a chance to learn the role of responsible citizen which is said to be so high on the nation's agenda? This is a crucial issue to be addressed in personal/social education modules so that children can be informed of their rights in law and given opportunity and information which enables them to exercise them. Education is intended to set children free, not to keep them in passive ignorance of what they need to know.

I offer the following as points for further discussion; between parents and their children, between teachers and children, between governors and children. There is room for considerable discretion and some schools already give far greater access to decision-making than others. With increasing freedom at the local level there is plenty of scope for experiment and mutual sharing of experience. Much depends on our willingness to try. These ideas may provide a limited framework within which to look for modest changes.

Complaints procedures

Pupil grievances
Establishments caring for children run by the local authority or by voluntary organizations must have established complaints procedures which enable children to expose situations where they may be subject to abuse, discrimination or injustice. Residential schools must offer children access to external procedures, independent of the school, which should be published and easily accessible. What does a child do if he wishes to complain about his treatment in an LEA or grant maintained day school? Some stay away or cause trouble because they don't know how else to call attention to their disquiet. In theory, they should complain to their parents, who are responsible for taking up the matter with the school.

This will often work. If the parent is skilled in complaining and the school welcomes such involvement, this may be more than sufficient. But the child may have little confidence in such a process; they may fear for the consequences if they are seen as making trouble; the parent may not take up the matter or may lack the necessary skill to do so. They may act inappropriately towards school staff, thereby compounding the child's lack of trust in the whole business. There may be an automatic assumption by everyone that the complaint cannot possibly be justified and little objective analysis made. With decision-making increasingly concentrated within the school and with the LEA as a relatively powerless onlooker, there is a real risk that quite genuine causes of complaint will be ignored or covered over.

Independent procedures
It seems to me to be in the best interests of everybody, including governors and teachers, to have some independent process available. No school wants a scandal in which they are subsequently seen to have taken no action where there were real grounds for doing so. No school wants a complaint against a teacher of a minor kind to be automatically investigated under child protection procedures, with all the consequent implications, because no routine process is available as an alternative.

There are some cases which must be investigated in this way – teachers do occasionally physically or sexually abuse children in their care and all schools/LEAs must have procedures to deal with such accusations. No other way of doing things should undermine the need for such an approach in such extreme situations.

But most complaints are not of this kind even though they still may give genuine cause for concern. Children may be subject to racist remarks or active discrimination; they may feel that the school has taken no action to deal with bullying or that unreasonable physical restraint has been used against them. They may feel they have been treated unfairly in a disciplinary matter with no right of appeal to anyone else. They may have genuine criticisms of their teacher's behaviour. If there is no process which can be put into place in such circumstances other than informal and internal methods with no independent right of redress, many children will not accept that they have been properly heard. This tends to store up resentment and often creates even more problems later, both for the child and for the school.

The role of the EWO/ESW

Education welfare officers/social workers often play the role of independent arbiter/peacemaker and the continued commitment of the Government to ensuring that they are funded from outside delegated budgets is to be much welcomed in this context. LEAs have a responsibility to make such a service available to all children and their parents, whether or not they maintain the school. EWOs/ ESWs are not simply agents of the school, even if many parents, and some headteachers, see them in this way. Their client is the child; school staff are their professional colleagues.

Any independence which they have would be severely undermined if they were answerable directly to the headteacher or the governors. Their concern will be only to promote the welfare of the child. They should be allowed to make sure that children are given a proper voice in any issue of complaint and will seek to work with all those involved to implement a solution. All sides may need to accept that they 'belong' to no one. Schools might want to make it clear to parents and children that this facility is available if problems arise, or they may wish to advertise some other person as being available for this purpose, including promoting 'helpline' numbers and organizations seeking to promote children's rights (see Appendix 2).

A governor for pupils?

Models of representation

Children cannot be governors of their schools, though a few admit them as observers. This general lack of access to the decision-makers no longer seems in keeping with the spirit of the Children Act and schools may wish to experiment with ways of opening up the governing body to closer dialogue with those for whom they are responsible. There are a number of ways of doing this, from suggestion boxes to governors actually spending time getting to know the children and listening to what they have to say. But probably one of the best ways is to ensure that at least one member of the governing body understands their particular role to be expressing the wishes and feelings of the pupils.

We have governors to represent the interests of parents, teachers and the wider community. It seems incredible that there may be no one who can speak for the pupils or take a perspective on decision-making which sees things from their point of view. Perhaps one of the parent-governors might take on this responsibility and seek ways of eliciting the children's opinions about the school. This can only improve the governors' effectiveness. For example, in my experience at least, children are by far the best judges of their teachers' competence and any question concerning appraisal of teacher performance cannot possibly be considered without including the views of those who spend all day with them.

Perhaps the children might help to choose such a person in some way, by, for example, inviting a parent in whom they have confidence to stand as a parent-governor on their behalf. This person could then report regularly through a newsletter or by meeting with pupil representatives to feed back the results of their actions. None of this should undermine the authority of either the headteacher or the governors but it should at least ensure that the interests of the 'customers' are not overlooked.

School councils

Formally elected bodies have gone in and out of fashion over the years and there is wide diversity in practice across the country. They often fail because the pupils are said to lack any interest in them – though this may be because experience has taught them that no one takes much notice of what they say. It would seem entirely reasonable that proposed changes which the governing body is seeking to make, eg, to policy on uniform or changes to the school day, should be fully discussed with those who are going to be most directly affected. Their views can then be fed back to those who carry the final responsibility, either directly or through their representative governor.

Occasionally children may actually have a good idea; they may see the solution to a problem which has been overlooked by those who do not view the school as they do. Any school which wants its pupils to identify with its aims and priorities will wish to take every available opportunity of moving forward through consultation. How can children be expected to fall in line otherwise? Do *we* willingly go along with things which others have said that we must do without asking us first?

Individual rights

Denying basic justice
Children have few rights at school. They have no right to see their personal files until they are 16 and even then few schools seem to make the facility available, so they have little opportunity to challenge what others have said about them. They cannot appeal in their own right against their exclusion; they are dependent on their parents doing so. Even then they have no automatic right to be present at any hearing, which may also not include any 'independent' person to represent their views. Increasingly some children seem to be expected to accept the school's rules with little scope for negotiation in the light of their individual circumstances or risk exclusion on the grounds that they have broken the 'contract of admission' on which their place was offered.

It is parents, not children, who have a right of appeal to the new tribunal if there are disputes over the provision of special education. Neither do children have any say in determining whether or not their school should remain under LEA control. They have no right to challenge the refusal of a school to admit them nor to question the alternative provision which is made if no school is willing to take them in.

LEAs, headteachers and governors have the right under the Education (No 2) Act 1986 to forbid 'junior pupils' from pursuing 'partisan political activities'. This is effectively discrimination on grounds of age as no such prohibition exists for older pupils, though few schools actively encourage such a thing (some on the quite reasonable grounds that it may foster extremism and racism). A late amendment to the 1993 Education Act has, at long last, removed the power of governors to veto sex education entirely, but parents may still request that their children be withdrawn. There is no requirement to consult the child concerned and so extensive restrictions can still be placed on his right to information without the child's voice being heard.

Neither do children have any right to control their participation in religious worship/education or to ensure that their religious views/traditions are respected at school. Again, unlike the Children Act, education law only recognizes the rights of parents in this area. Children are continually subject to the decisions of adults, as if we were still working within a framework which expects them to be seen and not heard like Victorian ornaments!

A right to be heard

Yet a child's whole school career is riddled with duties: to attend (for 11 years!), to do their homework, to be on time, to follow the rules, to wear what they are told to wear, even not to have their hair cut in certain ways. Of course they are young and schools might become anarchic if they were given more freedom (though they might not), but this represents all of the responsibilities with *none* of the power. Surely there is room for some shift in emphasis without the whole fabric of the school being threatened? If not, everybody must be operating on a knife-edge which suggests that something is seriously wrong.

Ironically, as we have seen already, children will be taken much more seriously and given far more chance to participate when they come to the attention of outside agencies. If an EWO/ESW is making an assessment for an education supervision order because the child's attendance is poor, he or she will be going out of their way to make sure that they are listening to what he wants to say, even if they disagree with him. Everyone will probably be asked in court if it has been done. The child has the right to go back to the court and ask for the order to be removed on the grounds that promises made at the beginning have not been kept. During the course of the order the supervisor has a duty to take the child's wishes and feelings into account before making any changes or issuing a 'direction'.

If the order failed and the child ended up on a care order, he would have even greater rights and those looking after him would be required to facilitate his active involvement in decision-making. Sadly some children only get into these processes because no one has listened properly before, in their family, at school or elsewhere – that is why the problem has arisen. (The Children's Society has used a wonderful poster showing a child saying: 'What I need is a good listening to'.) Progress is often made, not only because of the authority which orders bring but because everyone is now required to follow Children Act principles which did not apply before.

A pupil's charter
Would it not be a good idea for schools to agree some kind of 'pupil's charter'? (This is not an entirely original suggestion. At least one such charter has already been drawn up by the Northumberland School Governors' Association, although it concentrates on wider issues rather than pupils' rights as individuals. The Centre for the Study of Comprehensive Schools has drawn up an Action Guide about home/school partnership which stresses that children must be part of any such arrangements in their own right.)

We seem to have charters for everyone else these days, but none for children (though it must be said that there is none for teachers either!). We all know what a child is expected to do when they are admitted to a school. But what is the school offering to them? What commitments are the staff and the governing body prepared to make to them as the day-to-day 'customers'?

Such a charter might cover the quality of the educational provision on offer, rights to privacy and confidentiality, opportunities for pastoral care, access to decision-making, consultation and complaints procedures, commitments to anti-discriminatory practice, etc. It could lay down standard procedures to be followed in the event of a dispute and, as with other Charters, could be used by pupils and parents *together* as a means by which the school could be evaluated. Why are children by-passed in all the provision which is now in place for making comparisons and judgements about a school's quality? Will children's perceptions be sought on whether theirs is a 'failing' school under the new Education Association procedures? Somehow I doubt it. What a missed opportunity to involve them in learning the skills of responsible partnership! When are we going to start taking our pupils seriously?

CONCLUSION

The Children Act is supposed to represent a major milestone in the promotion of the welfare of children in our society. Many people are already disappointed in it. Some argue that it has been virtually strangled at birth by contradictory guidance. Some of its provisions are being overlooked or ignored by policy makers and practitioners in local and central government. Courts do not always seem committed to its principles and there seems to have been something of a conspiracy of silence in the legal profession and elsewhere not to broadcast its implications too widely. There appears even to be some embarrassment that such a humane and enlightened piece of legislation may have slipped through unnoticed and a very real risk that it will never have the impact which was intended.

I am generally more hopeful than that. But it is high time for the cat to be let out of the bag, for the sake of the children who need the Act's commitment to their welfare to be made more manifest. Schools are in an ideal position to help make it happen and must share the blame if it never does.

Appendix 1

Whole School Policies

There is never a good time for schools and LEAs to be facing yet more new information. Governors and teachers are already reeling from the effects of the national curriculum, the controversy over new testing arrangements, local financial management and the power to become grant maintained. All these mean that agendas are already very full and that there is less time than ever for standing back and evaluating whether or not the school is meeting the welfare needs of children and their parents.

This may seem at first thought to be a peripheral issue. Yet my experience has been that, when confronted with the issues in a managed way, governors have been immensely interested and keen to participate in the discussion. The module of training on the Children Act which is offered in the Staffordshire training programme has been the most popular of them all.

This is probably because there has been a whole LEA approach to the Act which has meant that such issues were not seen simply as the concern of the Welfare Service. An introductory booklet on the educational implications of the Act and the new terms it uses was sent initially to all heads and chairs of governors. Follow-up training was then offered through the Inspectorate, first direct to secondary heads and then to deputies and senior teachers using GEST (Grants for Education Support and Training) funding. Some of these involved professionals from other agencies, especially social workers from child protection teams.

Further events for junior heads were then demanded, but the main means of training has been through events at individual school or pyramid level, delivered by specialist officers from within the Education Welfare Service. Virtually all of the pastoral staff in senior schools have attended at least one 'twilight' briefing session or training day of this kind, many of which were thrown open to their junior colleagues.

The emphasis has been to stress the two dimensions of Children Act implementation in schools: pastoral *practice* for staff and school *policy* for governors. Four themes from the Act were identified as the key issues in order to avoid over-burdening recipients with detail: the welfare of the child, parental responsibility, attendance and absence and child protection. Study-packs for governors and handouts for teachers, making extensive use of the free DoH booklets, were also made available.

Governors were then invited to draw up whole school policies in response to the Act in order to ensure some consistency of practice. Although it is very important that teaching staff become skilled in pastoral practice in line with the Act's expectations, it is even more important that those responsible for school management recognize the importance of these tasks and make adequate provision for them to be carried out. Some of them *must* be a matter of policy (eg, child protection); in other situations (eg, the involvement of 'absent' parents) it is highly desirable that they are not simply left to the discretion and whim of individuals or mistakes may be made for which governors will be ultimately accountable.

The following policy discussion documents are offered as guidance for others who wish to encourage something similar. They relate to the situation for which they were created and should not simply be lifted wholesale into other contexts. They may, however, enable others to go through a similar process by highlighting in summary form the questions with which this book has been concerned. For busy governors and headteachers it may be best to start here by selecting the issue which is of primary importance to you and then work backwards by gathering more detail about that issue in response to the following outlines. You will need to formulate your own answers, but most of the questions are in here somewhere!

THE WELFARE OF THE CHILD

The Children Act has placed the welfare of the child at the centre of legal proceedings about children (see the 'welfare checklist' s1(3)). The Act is also a wider challenge to all professionals/agencies regarding the need to promote children's welfare and support parents in their parental responsibility. Children do not learn effectively when they are distressed or disadvantaged and schools are obviously concerned to be seen by parents and children as caring for their needs. The Act affirms that children are individuals in their own right, who should be consulted and listened to when decisions are being made about them.

Whole school policy issues include:

Is there a procedure for children to use if they have a complaint? Could one of the governors be available directly to children if they wish to make a complaint about their treatment by staff/other pupils? Is there any independent element in these procedures from outside the school?

Are children consulted about important issues which affect them? Are there mechanisms which allow their voice to be heard (eg, in exclusions)? Does the curriculum include opportunities for pupils to be made aware of their rights? Are they aware of the UN Convention?

What statements need to be in the school's brochure to demonstrate an active commitment to promoting children's welfare? Areas might include:

- the school's response to allegations/incidents of bullying;
- equal opportunities policies, including positive policies to promote religious/cultural/racial understanding, with clear sanctions against racism by staff or pupils;
- the school's pastoral system – all staff or specialists?
- commitments to promote the involvement of children with disabilities or special educational needs.

Is one of the areas in which the school is aiming to market itself, the quality of its pastoral care, even for those children who need extra help or who present challenging behaviour? Has this been discussed with the teaching staff/support services/parents/children?

The Children Act envisages a wider range of out-of-school activities for 'children in need'. What attitude does the governing body take to the use of school premises for such activities in the evenings/weekends/school holidays?

Some children will not easily fit into the usual systems or will raise extra complications. What policies might be needed on:

- children who are being 'looked after' by the local authority;
- children with behavioural problems/at risk of exclusion;
- children with poor attendance
- travelling children?

Is the governing body prepared to say that the school is open to all these groups? What resources are needed to support the teaching staff?

PARENTAL RESPONSIBILITY

Parents are crucial partners in the delivery of education. No school can function without seeking to promote positive relationships with parents. In some situations schools are under legal obligations to report to parents, consult them or even act in response to their expressed wishes. Children do best when their parents are welcomed and when any barriers are broken down.

The Children Act redefined the term 'parent' within *all* other education legislation (Schedule 13.10(1D)). 'Parent' now includes:

- all those who have 'parental responsibility' for a child, (whether or not they are a natural parent and whether or not they live with the child);
- any person who has the care of the child.

Whole school policy issues include:

What procedure does the school have for collecting information about the parents of registered pupils? Under the Pupil's Registration (Amendment) Regulations 1988, governors must make reasonable efforts to draw up accurate lists of parents and their addresses. How will this process be handled, especially where the information is of a sensitive nature or parents are in dispute? What training has been given to teaching and non-teaching staff? What procedures have been agreed for them to follow? How are parents being informed of the issues?

What policy has the school established for dealing with 'absent' parents (ie, people with parental responsibility who do not live with the child)? They are entitled:

- to receive reports/information on their child's progress;
- to be consulted about important decisions;
- to receive brochures, opportunities to vote in ballots etc;
- to consultation with teaching staff.

How are their wishes regarding these rights being identified?

What are the arrangements for the giving of parental consent? Does the governing body wish to encourage the signature of someone with parental responsibility for important decisions? What information is needed for parents? What amendments are needed on forms etc?

The Children Act affirms that parents are the key agents for delivering the welfare of children and that professionals should work in partnership with them. How are parents involved in the management of their children's education? What special procedures might be needed where:

- there are language difficulties;
- parents have literacy/reading problems;
- parents are unco-operative or hostile;
- parents find coming to the school difficult?

One of the aims of the Education Welfare/Education Social Work Service is to enable better communication between home and school. When did the governing body last discuss the responsibilities of their EWO/ESW and receive information on their work?

ATTENDANCE AND ABSENCE

The Government has made it clear that there is not much point in reforming the curriculum and raising standards within schools if children are not there to benefit. The Children Act has changed the legal basis on which the LEA may take action in the courts by introducing the education supervision order, to be applied for and managed by education welfare officers/education social workers (s36). The balance of responsibility is changing with the shift of resources towards schools. The LEA continues to play a vital role, but schools are increasingly expected to establish policies in this area. There is much a school can do to promote better attendance by working in partnership with EWOs/ESWs, parents and with children themselves.

Whole school policy issues include:

What is the role of the EWO/ESW in the overall strategy of the school to promote attendance/investigate absence? How aware are the governors of their work and what reporting mechanisms exist? Are referral procedures clear and properly used? Where does the balance of responsibilities lie?

What internal procedures does the school have for the initial investigation of absences? Who is responsible for ensuring that they are carried out? How much of this responsibility falls on secretarial/

clerical staff who may need proper training/support? Are mechanisms in place to detect and prevent 'internal truancy' after children have registered?

What policy have the governors laid down regarding 'authorized' and 'unauthorized' absence, or is it all a matter of individual discretion? The definitions used will have a significant effect on the power of the LEA to act in the courts. Are the criteria known to and understood by teachers, parents and children? What guidance do staff have concerning good practice? Is the school fulfilling its legal requirement to publish its rates of unauthorized absence (Education (School Performance Information) (No 2) Regulations 1993)?

What procedures have been given to parents regarding absence and lateness? What does it say in the school's brochure? Is the headteacher's discretionary power (eg, over family holidays in term time) clearly defined and properly carried out? Are parents aware of their legal obligations?

The Children Act expects all agencies to work together on the basis of agreement and partnership and only to use the courts when no other avenues are appropriate. Governing bodies should make it clear to staff that procedures involving written agreements, consultation etc. must be responded to positively. What commitments are the governing body prepared to make in order to encourage such arrangements to be successful? How are they encouraging creative relationships between home and school? How are they supporting the work of their EWO/ESW?

Education supervision orders will require commitment by the school if they are to succeed. The child concerned may need extra assistance, staff will be required for meetings, reports will need to be provided. Extra resources to enable the child to benefit fully from education may be asked for by the supervisor, eg, help with the costs of a school visit or school clothing. How will governors react?

CHILD PROTECTION

Child protection is a vital area of inter-agency responsibility in which schools are bound by statutory legislation, Government guidance under the Children Act such as *Working Together* and the local procedures agreed by the appropriate Area Child Protection Committee (ACPC). All schools contain children who may become the subject of a child protection investigation and all schools should be promoting positive policies which aim to protect children from potential abuse. Staff must be made aware by governors that standard procedures must be followed and that the exercise of discretion without proper consultation is strictly limited.

The Children Act requires schools/LEAs to co-operate with the SSD on these issues (Part V). Timetables may be very quick as delay is prejudicial to the child's welfare. The attendance of key staff at case conferences will be expected. Governors are ultimately responsible for ensuring that inter-agency requirements are met.

Whole school policy issues include:

Are governors aware of the local ACPC procedures? Where is the handbook of guidance which sets down the responsibilities of teaching staff? Have staff been trained appropriately? Is information which is sent to the school by the ACPC/LEA passed on to those who need to know it?

Are the governors aware of who the LEA has nominated as the responsible member of staff for child protection issues? What is their role? Is policy needed which would enable procedures to be followed in their absence?

Does the governing body recognize that playing their full part in child protection issues may have resource implications? These include:

- providing cover for staff required to attend case conferences, sometimes at short notice;
- providing secretarial support for the production of written reports;
- resourcing training for key staff/procedural handbooks.

What procedures exist should the LEA/SSD need to obtain information about a child during the school holidays, especially in July/ August?

Does the headteacher report to the governors on his/her involvement in child protection issues? Are confidential procedures working properly? How can governors best be informed, but in ways which do not compromise confidentiality, especially where other parents are concerned?

Does the school have a positive policy of promoting discussion about child protection issues with pupils, especially as part of PSE modules? Older children in particular may be helped to protect themselves and even younger children may need to be aware of some of the issues. Are there 'safe' places within the school pro-gramme where children who are looking for an opportunity to disclose may identify an adult in whom they can trust? How is the school promoting such open relationships in which children can feel confident to express themselves without condemnation?

Appendix 2

For Further Information

This list is by no means exhaustive, but it may provide further opportunities to follow up certain aspects of the Children Act in schools.

GOVERNMENT PUBLICATIONS

The Children Act 1989. HMSO (1989)
(Should be available in reference libraries)

At the point of writing, no guidance on the Children Act has been issued by the Department for Education, other than joint guidance with the Department of Health as follows:

The Children Act 1989, Guidance and Regulations, Vol 5, HMSO (1991)
   (Independent Schools)
The Children Act 1989, Guidance and Regulations, Vol 7, HMSO (1991)
   (including Education Supervision Orders – Chapter 3)
Working Together under the Children Act 1989, HMSO (1991) (Child
   Protection)

The Department of Health publishes a series of free information leaflets – all available in English only:

   CAG 1 *The Children Act and Local Authorities*
   CAG 2 *The Children Act and the Courts – A Guide for Parents*
   CAG 3 *The Children Act and You – A Guide for Young People*
   CAG 4 *The Children Act and Day Care*
   CAG 5 *Getting Help from Social Services*
   CAG 6 *The Children Act and the Courts – Young People's Version*
   CAG 7 *Living away from Home: Your Rights – A Guide for Young
       People*

These are available from: Department of Health Stores, Health Publications Unit, No 2 site, Manchester Road, Heywood, Lancashire OL10 2PZ.

THE OPEN UNIVERSITY

The Children Act 1989: A Guide for the Education Service (P558Y, 1991) (produced at the request of the DfE but not formal guidance as such)

The OU also publishes comprehensive training packages on the Act. Though these are not particularly useful for schools, they have been used by local authorities and magistrates as the basis of their training and so copies may be available locally on loan.

BOOKS

White, R, Carr, P and Lowe, N (1990) *A Guide to the Children Act 1989*. Butterworths. (Contains full text of the Act and a very useful, readable commentary.)
Dimmock, B (ed) (1992) *A Step in Both Directions? The Impact of the Children Act on Stepfamilies*. STEPFAMILY.
Freeman, M (1992) *Children, their families and the Law*. Macmillan.

TEACHERS' GUIDES

The Children Act and the Teacher, 8-page guide published by AMMA, 7 Northumberland St, London WC2N 5DA, February 1992.
'The Children Act 1989', *The Head's Legal Guide*, March 1992 (pp 483–93).
Webb, S. 'Helping Troubled and Troublesome Children'. *Croner's Head Teachers Bulletin*, November 1992. (An excellent article on Children Act principles in practice.)

ORGANIZATIONS

These are all known to be interested in Children Act issues:

Advisory Centre for Education
1b Aberdeen Studios
22–24 Highbury Grove
London N5 2EA
071 354 8318

Children's Legal Centre
20 Compton Terrace
London N1 2UN
071 359 9392

Children's Rights Development
  Unit
235 Shaftesbury Avenue
London WC2H 8EL
071 240 4449
(monitors the UN Convention in
  the UK)

Family Rights Group
The Print House
18 Ashwin Street
London E8 3DL
071 923 2628

National Association of Young
  People in Care
20 Compton Terrace
London N1 2UN
071 226 7102

National Children's Bureau
8 Wakley Street
London EC1V 7QE
071 278 9441

STEPFAMILY
The National Stepfamily
  Association
72 Willesden Lane
London NW6 7TA
071 372 0844

HELPLINES/ADVICE LINES

Childline 0800 1111
NSPCC Child Protection Line 0800 800500
Children's Legal Centre 071 359 6251 (2–5pm Mon–Fri)
Advice and Advocacy Service for Children 0800 616101
Family Rights Group 071 249 0008 (Mon and Fri am, Weds pm)

Index